TERESA SHIEL

SWEET HUNGER

DEVELOPING AN APPETITE FOR GOD

A PERSONAL OR GROUP BIBLE STUDY

Write THE VISION.NET

SWEET HUNGER
DEVELOPING AN APPETITE FOR GOD

Printed in the USA

ISBN: 978-0-9910012-9-3

Published by Write the Vision | Columbia, Missouri   *Write*
THE VISION.NET

To Contact the Author:

www.TeresaShieldsParker.com

D E D I C A T I O N

*To every person who desires to love
God more than a cookie,
but has no idea how to go about doing that.
To those whose deepest desire is to crave God's presence,
but the brownies get in the way.
God sees you as beautiful and is waiting for you
to ask Him for help.
You are weak, that is true,
but in Him you are stronger than strong.
He is drawing you near.
He's beckoning you to come to Him.
He's calling your name right now.
Your deepest desires have been answered
not in the sweet foods that tempt you,
but in your soul's deep yearning for
more of the reality of God.
It is the sweetest of all hungers
and only God can satisfy it.*

When God fulfills your longing,
sweetness fills your soul.
PROVERBS 13:19 TPT

FOREWORD

Teresa Shields Parker has an incredible story of God leading her to lose over 260 pounds. Being her pastor for many years I have had the privilege of watching the development of her Sweet Series of books move from idea to publication. This book, the sixth in the series, brings together her story with eight Bible studies you can use for personal or group discussion. God has truly used her to touch many lives through her writing, coaching and speaking.

What I love about Teresa's testimony is that she identifies a rarely discussed issue in the Church realm: unhealthy eating habits. I can say as a pastor I have seldom mentioned the sin of gluttony and certainly have never made a whole sermon about that issue.

Teresa, however, does address gluttony, as well as sugar and food addictions. With two-thirds of Americans overweight and obese it is a huge issue the Church as a whole is largely ignoring.

In *Sweet Hunger: Developing An Appetite for God*, Teresa takes normal everyday Bible stories most Christians are familiar with and helps us understand how God uses food to symbolize our need for His presence in our lives.

Of all the things people put on the "throne of their hearts", our stomachs could possibly be the most damning. The line Teresa draws is not one of condemnation, but of exhortation from a lifetime of experience with the stronghold we many times allow certain foods to have in our lives.

She was seeking satisfaction not from Jesus, but from sugar and comfort foods. This addiction controlled her and limited her in so many ways. The sweet freedom she finally experienced came when the Holy Spirit revealed the truth of this idolatry to her.

In Teresa's books you'll not find a get-thin-quick scheme or a fad diet, but rather a wonderful story of how the sweet grace of God came to her in unexpected ways and helped her walk out her journey. Her story will encourage you, but even more, the insights, thoughts and questions she shares will help you delve more deeply into the issues which may also have you bound.

Whether you have an issue with food or not, this book, along with the content, questions and activities, will lead you on a journey of longing for the sweetness only God can provide in your life.

Journey with Teresa into the very presence of God as you learn to develop a never-ending appetite for Him.

Jeremy Risner, Lead Pastor
C2 Church, Columbia, MO

AUTHOR'S NOTE

'␣ve made a firm decision to allow God to change my appetite. No longer do I crave the sweet foods I desired for most of my life. Today, I crave fellowship with God. I want to develop an even more ravenous appetite for Him, a hunger for the sweetest thing of all—the overwhelming, never-ending presence of my Creator, sitting in the heavenly realms with Him, even right here on earth.

When God realized I was serious about learning how I can be as hungry for Him as I am for certain foods, He began teaching me. He showed me how mentions of food throughout Scripture relate to seeking Him and His presence.

As I studied, God opened His Word in new ways to me. Everywhere I looked I saw how God uses examples of food to relate to Himself. I began to see what I was learning wasn't just for me. It was information for you as well.

In the pages of this book you will read some familiar and some not so familiar Biblical stories. As always, I have more questions than answers after I study God's Word. However, I believe it is only when I ask God the questions burning in my heart that I will find answers specifically designed for me. If I can lead you to ask those same questions, I believe you will also discover your own personal answers.

When we experience truth for ourselves we begin to really know and own the truth. Jesus told the Jewish believers, "Then you will experience for yourselves the truth, and the truth will free you."[1]

QUESTIONS AND ACTIVITIES

At the end of each chapter you will find a list of questions with space to jot down answers. If you're like me and can't read your own handwriting, you may want to type your answers and keep them in a folder on your computer to refer to.

Every question will lead you deeper spiritually if you have the courage to have a real conversation with God. Leave your questions in His capable hands and allow His answers to come through Scripture, a song, a message, a book, a friend or an observation in nature. He will drop an insight or an answer into your heart when you least expect it.

I've developed an honest and open relationship with Him. I'm not afraid to ask Him anything, to tell Him the truth of how I feel or to spill my guts in His presence. Many times I do that by journaling a conversation I've had with Him. Sometimes it's just Him speaking in my mind or heart after I've asked Him a question. He always answers. I just have to be listening.

Some days, it is a praise music day. Sometimes it involves forcing myself to stop and just shut out all sound and acknowledge God's presence in the silence and solitude. Other

CONTENTS

Suspended In Grace

Thump, ka-thump, scratch, scrunch.
Rhythm disrupted.
Life skips a beat.
Rats racing in a maze.
Cats waiting to pounce.
Dogs panting with glee.
The merry-go-round continues.
Pleasant, then faster, faster,
'Til the children scream and hang on in fear.
Somewhere, somehow,
I am on hold.
Suspended, upended,
Dismembered and wondering.

I fall on my face writhing in my sweat.
Anguish, fear, overwhelm, frustration.
Then I hear it, starting softly,
Building, cascading to highs
And lows, loud then soft,
Higher, higher to a momentous crescendo
Of light and beauty and sound.
Connecting.
Knowing.
Understanding.

In the presence of Wisdom.
Nothing and everything changes
In one moment of surrender.

Thump, thump, thump, thump.
Rhythm in sync.
Clear and distinct.
All of life is but a song.
Children living free.
Moms hugging tight.
Dads steadily strong.
The carnival continues.
Pleasant afternoon at the park.
The children squeal in delight.
I am here now.
Suspended in Grace.
Holding tight. He never fails.

INTRODUCTION

F or more of my life than not, I have felt like I was hungry, like there was an empty hole inside me that needed to be filled. At an early age, I began filling that void with the thing that was acceptable and even encouraged—food.

Growing up in a Christian home in the 50's and 60's there were a lot of don'ts. One thing that wasn't on the don't list was eating things like pies, cakes, cookies, donuts, ice cream and brownies. In all of life's ups and downs there was one thing I learned that I could count on and that was food, especially foods with high carbohydrate content.

I found eating these kinds of foods would calm me when I was stressed, angry, sad, lonely, bored or overwhelmed with life, even if just for a moment. It was also the way I celebrated. It was the one thing I could always count on to make me happy or what I perceived as happy.

The wonderful cooks in my family, especially my grandmother, made eating a delight. Going to Grandma's house was a day long, weekend-long or week-long food fest. I loved spending time there. It was the food, but it was also because I knew she loved me unconditionally. As a result wonderful desserts and comfort foods became enmeshed with love and Grandma. They were inseparable in my mind.

COMFORTER

Growing up in a Christian home, one might think I would have first learned that the Holy Spirit is the Comforter.[1] I knew this in theory. I'd heard sermons preached. I can remember my father turning to God every day and finding solace in prayer and reading the Bible. It just never connected in my mind with how God's presence could help me understand and deal with my emotions. It really never crossed my mind to even assume I could bother God with the petty things that stressed me out. I mean, did He really care that I put all my spelling words on the wrong test in second grade, got an "F" and blubbered all over myself in front of a classroom full of well-dressed snobby peers?

> It really never crossed my mind to even assume I could bother God with the petty things that stressed me out.

I would have never thought to bother God with such an issue, especially not when cookies were readily at hand when I got home at the end of the school day.

God, though, does care and does want to be bothered with my issues and problems. Food is wonderful, but it can never replace God's presence in my life. All through the Bible, God uses food, an everyday substance, to explain how His presence is always with us. He should be inside us, just like the food we eat and the water we drink. As often as we eat, we should remember Him. And when we face difficulties, even though we might need physical sustenance, it's always His presence that helps us win the battle.

There are so many wonderful Bible stories that tell us we need to develop a hearty appetite, not for food that is here today and gone tomorrow, but for God. He is really all we need. He fulfills us. He gives us strength. He is our sustenance. He is the Bread of Life.

CATAPULTED FROM COMFORT

We don't escape our comfort zones until something catapults us out of them. My comfort zone definitely became the way I ate. It quickly morphed into being very uncomfortable when I gained up to 430 pounds. Even though a cardiac surgeon told me I only had five years to live if I didn't lose weight and keep it off, I couldn't give up my comfort foods.

I needed an eject button from this deadly lifestyle, but I just couldn't bring myself to push it. God put me in that ejection seat anyway just to see what would happen.

When a mentor of mine said the words, "Alcohol is one molecule away from sugar. Alcohol is liquid sugar," my entire world shifted and I felt like I had been shot out of a cannon. In that moment, everything that had ever happened in my life snapped together like a magnetic puzzle. I saw every diet I had been on where I had willingly abstained from sugar, starches and breads and ate meat, veggies and proteins. I saw how those plans had worked until I went off them and rewarded myself with Mamaw's oatmeal cake.

I knew the signs. If I kept lying to myself and kept going on like there was no tomorrow, there would be no tomorrow for me, at least not here on earth. My carefully constructed go-to source to eradicate any emotional discomfort had just been totally rearranged by the words my mentor spoke. My comfort zone had suddenly become very uncomfortable and I was more than ready to escape it. I began the process of giving up sugar.[2] Only this time, I laid myself on the altar. I knew my tendencies and my past history. I knew I could not do this without God's help.

Sugar was my kryptonite, the thing that made me weak.

That day, the God's words to the Apostle Paul became my mantra. "My grace is enough. It's all you need. My power is made complete in your weakness."[3] Part of this was acknowledging that sugar was my kryptonite, the thing that made me weak. I needed God's strength to lead me step-by-step in how to walk out my journey.

As He began leading me, I joined a group of people with similar issues to mine. It was led by a coach who understood food addiction. Soon I began to lose weight.[4]

Now, after losing 260 pounds, I feel so much better, free from the bondages of sugar cravings, free to be hungry or full[5] and free to be content with little or plenty.[6]

There were many emotional reasons why I ate. They had to do with how I tried to get my basic needs met when I was a child. Our basic needs are protection, provision, identity,

Need More Inspiration?

Draw a picture that symbolizes where you are now and where you want to be. It can be anything even a stick figure. No artistic ability needed.

ENDNOTES

1. John 14:26 KJV

2. For more about how to rid sugar from your life go to https://teresashield-sparker.com/kicksugar to access Teresa's FREE course.

3. 2 Cor. 12:9 MSG

4. For information about how to join Teresa's online weight loss coaching groups, Sweet Change or #KickWeight, go to https://TeresaShieldsParker.com/Sweet-Change/ or https://TeresaShieldsParker.com/KickWeight/.

5. Philippians 4:12 TPT

6. Philippians 4:12 NLT

7. To learn more about this process see Teresa's books, *Sweet Freedom: Losing Weight and Keeping It Off With God's Help* and *Sweet Freedom Study Guide*, both available on Amazon and at TeresaShieldsParker.com. *Sweet Grace: How I Lost 250 Pounds and Stopped Trying to Earn God's Favor* tells her story of physical weight loss. *Sweet Freedom* shared how she conquered emotional issues which led to spiritual lies and misbeliefs.

8. John 14:26-27 KJV

After giving instructions on how to properly observe the Lord's Supper, Paul told the church, "So, my friends, when you come together to the Lord's Table, be reverent and courteous with one another. If you're so hungry that you can't wait to be served, go home and get a sandwich. But by no means risk turning this meal into an eating and drinking binge or a family squabble. It is a spiritual meal—a love feast."[4]

In the 21st century we may be mortified by what Paul was describing as the celebration of the Lord's Supper. In most churches we have a small cracker and a sip of grape juice to remember Jesus' sacrifice for us.

Many New Testament churches, though, went all out for the Lord's Supper. It was more than a pinch and a sip. It was a meal fit for a king. Maybe they did that as a way to try to make it as meaningful as possible.

JESUS MAKES A POINT

Jesus didn't want an elaborate meal. He knew it would be His last intimate meal with just His disciples. His goal was to give them a way to remember Him every single day.

The time Jesus chose to celebrate His last meal with the disciples just happened to correspond with the Feast of the Passover, a time when the bread eaten was unleavened bread, to remind the Jewish people of the hasty way they left Egypt when running towards their freedom.

Although it doesn't specifically tell us that the bread eaten at the Last Supper was unleavened, it probably was since the time frame for the meal was either during the Feast of the Unleavened Bread or the Passover. The Greek word used for the bread Jesus broke, though, was "artos"[5] which is a general word for any kind of bread.[6]

There was nothing more ordinary to the Jewish culture than bread and wine. They had it with every meal. Jesus was giving the disciples a clear way to remember Him at least three times a day.

WHEN SHOULD WE REMEMBER JESUS?

When the resurrected Christ began walking with two of the disciples on the road to Emmaus, they recognized who they were with when He broke the bread.

"As they sat down to eat, He took the bread and blessed it. Then He broke it and gave it to them. Suddenly, their eyes were opened, and they recognized Him. And at that moment He disappeared!"[7]

It was in the way He broke the bread that they recognized Him as their risen Lord. Then they remembered His words as He took some bread, broke it in pieces and gave it to the disciples just several days before that time. "This is my body, which is given for you. This do in remembrance of Me."[8]

Suddenly these words that had seemed like a riddle back then made sense. It was a revelation moment. He had said to them, "I have been very eager to eat this Passover meal with you before my suffering begins. For I tell you I won't eat this meal again until its meaning is fulfilled in the Kingdom of God."[9]

He was crucified on a Roman cross. He died a sinless life and now they had seen with their own eyes that He had risen again. They hadn't known what to make of his death, but now it was clear. They had walked with the Messiah, the actual Son of God. He was risen! It was too glorious to contain.

NEVER THE SAME AGAIN

The normal breaking of bread at every meal would never again be the same. They would hold that memory with them always. They would remember Him often, every day, with every bite of bread they ate and every sip of wine or beverage they drank.[10] His presence would always be with them. No matter what happened they could not erase the memory of the Last Supper they had shared with the Master.

Meals with Jesus had been a necessity. They traveled the roads together walking and talking. They ate when they needed to, not worrying about the next meal because food seemed always to be the last thing on Jesus' mind.

WHERE DID JESUS GET FOOD?

They remembered what He had said at the well in Samaria. They had gone into town to get food. Jesus had sat down at the well to wait for them. When they returned He was talking to a Samaritan woman. They wondered if He had forgotten that Jews did not associate with Samaritans.

When she went running off, they tried to get Him to eat lunch. He gave one of His notorious puzzling responses. "I have a kind of food you know nothing about."[11] He was always doing that, talking in riddles.

They remembered talking with the other disciples asking if someone had already brought Him food. Then Jesus spoke up. "My nourishment comes from doing the will of God, who sent Me, and from finishing His work."[12]

He had said more about planting and harvesting, which they really didn't understand, but now it was all beginning to make sense. He was the Christ, the Son of the living God. They would have work to do to spread this news far and wide. This was what He meant by planting and harvesting. It wasn't crops He was talking about. It was souls.

Their nourishment would need to come from doing His will. Food, though, especially bread, would hold an extremely significant place in their memory and in their zeal for the gospel. It would remind them of the One they served with everything within them.

BREAKING BREAD TOGETHER

From that day on when the disciples shared a meal together and broke bread, I'm sure they paused and remembered that last night. It was one reason the early church loved to break bread together. The disciples had recounted the story of the Last Supper many times. "They continued steadfastly in the apostles' doctrine and fellowship, in the breaking of bread, and in prayers."[13]

By establishing the Last Supper, Jesus created a new ceremony. He was planning His memorial service, one that would be re-enacted countless times throughout history. No other memorial service comes close to this. Think of the number of times down through the ages this has been re-enacted each time remembering the One who died and rose again.

Each time we eat the bread we remember His broken body. He went willingly to the cross to provide a sinless sacrifice for us, a way for us to come to God. His blood was shed for our sins, a blood sacrifice of a spotless, perfect Lamb, the only Son of God.

Their nourishment would need to come from doing His will.

True belief in the Son of God is the only requirement for eternal life with God. It's a plan instituted by God from the beginning of time. "For God presented Jesus as the sacrifice for sin. People are made right with God when they believe that Jesus sacrificed His life, shedding His blood."[14]

Some of what Paul was trying to get across to the Corinthian Church was that the Lord's Supper should remind us that real life is found in Christ living in and through us.

Any time we sit down to eat a meal, we should remember His sacrifice for us. He was God, yes, but He willingly gave up His divinity when He came to earth.

"Let each of you look not only to his own interests, but also to the interests of others. Have this mind among yourselves, which is yours in Christ Jesus, who, though He was in the form of God, did not count equality with God a thing to be grasped, but emptied Himself, by taking the form of a servant, being born in the likeness of men. And being found in human form, He humbled Himself by becoming obedient to the point of death, even death on a cross."[15]

Jesus lived a sinless life as a man. He lived in the same limited form we do and yet, He was always in tune with His heavenly Father. It's impossible for us to understand. He had a human mother who knew better than anyone else that He was the Son of God. His earthly step-father knew His identity as well. They were hand-chosen by God to raise His only Son, to teach Him what He would need to know to finally step into His supreme calling—death.

KILLING THE PERFECT ONE

We don't know at what age Jesus realized that some day He would willingly give His life as a sacrifice for our sins, but at the age of 12 He had a wisdom beyond His years. He knew the scriptures. His father had taught Him well. If Jesus knew the scriptures and knew He was the son of a virgin, He likely knew His destiny from an early age.

He was the only man who ever conquered sin, completely. He was perfection and because of that humans killed Him. He was too intimidating. He was unbelievable in the fact that He went into towns and "healed them all."[16] Everyone was healed. People thought it was a trick, but it was no trick.

Jesus was God Himself come to earth. That same Jesus, who shed His blood for all mankind, accepted every person, no matter what they had done or hadn't done, and washed them white as snow in His blood. When Christ appeared, John said, "Behold the Lamb of God who takes away the sin of the world."[17]

Even the Old Testament speaks of this when it says, "Come now, let us reason together, says the Lord: though your sins are like scarlet, they shall be as white as snow; though they are red like crimson, they shall become like wool."[18]

The Bible is clear when it says, "All have sinned and fallen short of the glory of God."[19] Sin is just disobedience to God. It's failing to do what God asks us to do. This happens on a very personal level with each person because God works differently with each of His children.

There are, of course, some guidelines in scripture, but these are not exhaustive lists of do's and don'ts. When God gives us a directive and we stamp our feet like a two-year-old and say, "No," that is sin.

APPLICATION

Back in 1977, I was gaining weight. I probably weighed close to 250 pounds. I cried out to God and asked Him, "How can I move this mountain of flesh that has attached itself to my body?"

Jesus didn't hesitate to answer me, He said, "Stop eating sugar. Don't eat so much bread. Eat more meats, fruits and vegetables."

I said, "Nice plan, God. I could lose weight if I did that, but I can't do that so I'll try it my way." For the next 30 years I tried it my way, which resulted in the monumental weight gain. It wasn't until I repented of the sin of disobeying, surrendered to His way and followed what He showed me to do in obedience born of love for Him that the weight began to come off.

Food, or any substance or thing we think makes our emotional pain go away, is not the answer. Our hunger is not physical. It is spiritual. Until we understand that, take our failures and fall headlong into the arms of His sweet grace, we will always be struggling. Spiritual nourishment is found only in Jesus Christ.

My biggest failure was continuing in that lifestyle sin for at least 30 years. I see clearly why throughout Scripture God uses food as an illustration of His presence. God created us and designed us to get fuel from the plants and animals He also created.

In a perfect universe, life is a cycle that continues. Food is not meant for pleasure, but for sustaining life. We saw, though, even in the early churches there were difficulties with food, who gets served first, how much and when.

> Spiritual nourishment is found only in Jesus Christ.

By using the example of the broken bread and cup of wine as His body and blood Jesus was doing two things. First, He was asking us to remember Him every day at least as often as we eat. Second, He was reminding us to see what we eat as nourishment for doing Kingdom work, nothing else.

If we become mindful that every morsel we eat is like the broken body of Christ and every sip of beverage we drink is like His shed blood, it will change the way we live our lives.

He and He alone is our nourishment. He guides our lives if we will but remember Him as often as we eat and drink.

Questions

1. Be honest, have you ever gone to a church gathering just for the food? Think about how this can be both good and bad?

   _____

   _____

   _____

2. Why does the food pull us so much? What should be our focus? How can we make sure that is the focus rather than the foods we eat?

   _____

   _____

   _____

3. In 1 Corinthians 11:20-22 what is Paul so upset about? Why do you think this was happening in this church? What could be some underlying root causes of this? How does Paul want them to remedy the situation? What is the lesson here for you?

   _____

   _____

   _____

4. What was Jesus trying to get the disciples to remember during the Lord's Supper? See Luke 22:14-20.

_____

_____

_____

5. How is the way the disciples recognized Jesus in Luke 24:30-31 significant?

_____

_____

_____

6. How did Jesus change the way they looked at eating meals from then on? How should it change the way we look at eating meals? See 1 Corinthians 11:23-25 NLT.

_____

_____

_____

7. What food does Jesus have in John 4:32-34? How can we obtain that same food?

_____

_____

_____

8. What are we really commemorating during the celebration of the Lord's supper? See Philippians 2:4-8.

_____

_____

_____

9. What is sin to you? Why is surrendering a lifestyle sin so difficult? Romans 3:23, Isaiah 1:18 ESV.

_____

_____

_____

10. What has been your biggest sin? Have you laid that down? When? Does it still tempt you? How do you handle it today?

_____

_____

_____

Activity

SCRIPTURE: "And they have defeated him by the blood of the Lamb and by their testimony." —Revelation 12:11 NLT

SUPPLIES: Pen.

WRITE YOUR TESTIMONY: Write our your own personal testimony of when you became a Christian and what that means in your life. To get started, answer these three main questions:

1. When and how did you accept Jesus as your Savior? Has there been a time when you accepted Jesus' sacrifice for your sin and failed to follow Him?

_____

_____

_____

_____

2. What circumstances led you to accept Christ? Who was involved in helping lead you there?

_____

_____

_____

3. What difference has Jesus made in your life since? What difference does God's grace make in your life today? Does it mean you live a perfect life? What do you do when you realize you have been disobedient to God today?

_____

_____

_____

_____

_____

4. Now put this together and write your testimony on the next few pages provided. Your testimony should be short enough to share with someone on an elevator ride to the sixth floor. There are some additional scriptures that follow the blank pages if you wish to include any reference in your testimony.

5. After writing your testimony, read it aloud so you can hear it. Our words have a powerful effect on our lives. They can also impact others. No one can take your testimony from you. It is one of the best weapons we have to defeat the enemy. Share your testimony with someone else.

My Testimony

_____

_____

_____

_____

_____

_____

_____

_____

_____

_____

_____

_____

_____

_____

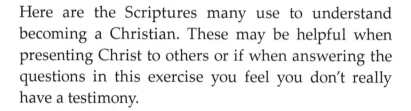

More Inspiration

Here are the Scriptures many use to understand becoming a Christian. These may be helpful when presenting Christ to others or if when answering the questions in this exercise you feel you don't really have a testimony.

- **Romans 3:23 NLT**—"For everyone has sinned; we all fall short of God's glorious standard."

- **Romans 3:25 NLT**—"For God presented Jesus as the sacrifice for sin. People are made right with God when they believe that Jesus sacrificed His life, shedding His blood."

- **Romans 6:23 NLT**—"For the wages of sin is death, but the free gift of God is eternal life through Christ Jesus our Lord.

- **John 3:16 NLT**—"For this is how God loved the world: He gave His one and only Son, so that everyone who believes in Him will not perish but have eternal life."

- **2 Corinthians 2:8-9 NLT**—"If you openly declare that Jesus is Lord and believe in your heart that God raised Him from the dead, you will be saved. For it is by believing in your heart that you are made right with God, and it is by openly declaring your faith that you are saved. "

- **Romans 10:9-10 NLT**—"If you openly declare that Jesus is Lord and believe in your heart that God raised Him from the dead, you will be saved. For it is by believing in your heart that you are made right with God, and it is by openly declaring your faith that you are saved."
- **1 John 1:9 NLT**—"If we confess our sins to Him, He is faithful and just to forgive us our sins and to cleanse us from all wickedness."

SIMPLE SALVATION PRAYER

Thank You Jesus for living a sinless life, for accepting a painful death on the cross as the sacrifice for my sin.

I repent of my sins and make a firm decision right now to invite You into my life as Savior and Lord.

I desire to follow You and Your ways. Teach me how to do that.

Thank You for Your grace which You have freely given me and which I do not deserve or understand.

Thank You for the deposit of Your Spirit in my heart.

My body is now a temple of the Holy Spirit.

I choose to love You and follow You all the days of my life. I love You Jesus. Amen.

ENDNOTES

1. 1 Corinthians 11:20-22 NIV
2. Acts 2:46-47 AMP
3. 1 Corinthians 11:20-22 MSG
4. 1 Corinthians 11:33-34 MSG
5. Matthew 26:26, Mark 14:22, Luke 22:19, 1 Corinthians 11:24 NIV
6. Butt, Kyle, M. Div. "Apologetics Press." *Apologetics Press.* N.p., 200e. Web. 18 Jan. 2017.
7. Luke 24:30-31 NLT
8. Luke 22:19 NLT
9. Luke 22:16 NLT
10. 1 Corinthians 11:23-25 ESV
11. John 4:32 NLT
12. John 4:34 NLT
13. Acts 2:42 NIV
14. John 3:16, Romans 3:25 NLT
15. Philippians 2:4-8 NLT
16. Luke 6:19 ESV
17. John 1:29 ESV
18. Isaiah 1:18 ESV
19. Romans 3:23 NLT

The Hunger Within

Everywhere, everyday people try to connect
to themselves and each other.
Something. Anything. Nothing
rings true until something becomes real and gives
Purpose. Meaning. Life.

Today I met a woman whom I've seen often,
but saw for the first time.
Seeing. Connecting. Knowing
the depths of a soul touched by
Fear. Turmoil. Despair.

I saw an emptiness waiting
for meaning to fill the expanse within.
Barren. Abandoned. Alone,
a soul longing to connect to a part of
Creation. Spirit. Design.

Deep within, my desperation escapes.
I am yearning to become all I can be.
Anxious. Eager. Hungry
for that which only an all-powerful God can
Complete. Fulfill. Satisfy.

CHAPTER 2

STARVING FOR GOD

Years ago, I attended a Christian-based weight loss program a friend was leading. The program had great spiritual teaching, but one of their premises was to eat when you are hungry and stop when you are full.

This was a huge problem for me. My broken metabolism would never clue my brain and body as to where "full" was. I constantly felt hungry. The woman who was the national coordinator was a small woman. I don't think she had ever had the monstrous weight issue I had.

She just had no idea of the battle those of us who are, or have been, super morbidly obese fight. When I was gaining weight faster than a bullet train, I never felt full. The program described full as a feeling of completion. I furrowed my eyebrows and said, "Huh?"

The other concept was that hunger was a "knowing feeling" in my stomach, even to where my stomach would begin to growl. My stomach gurgled a lot. I thought I was hungry all the time, but maybe it was from everything I fed it.

My local group leader was also thin. I was a challenge to her. Finally she said, "I want you to not eat until you feel a knowing in your stomach and it actually grumbles, not gurgles." When she saw the concerned look on my face, she said, "No, you will not die. You have plenty of storehouses of food in your body." In other words, "You are fat," but she was too nice to say it. She was also a nurse, so I trusted her wisdom.

I did as she said and after a day, I couldn't stand it. I downed a bag of cookies. In hindsight, I realize I was not actually hungry. I craved food constantly, but it was not physical hunger.

WHAT IS REAL HUNGER?

Here's a definition of hunger from the *Dictionary of Bible Themes*. "A state of emptiness, reflecting a lack of physical or spiritual food."[1] This recognizes that the physical aspect of human hunger, as well as the spiritual aspect, can only be met by the living God.

The book, *The Heavenly Man: The Remarkable True Story of Chinese Christian Brother Yun*, recounts the journey of Yun's escape from China to Germany in the midst of persecution and torture for his faith. At one point he was imprisoned for preaching the gospel in underground churches. While there he fasted for 74 days without food and water.

The guards were sure he would die, but he actually escaped this maximum security prison by simply walking away. He heard the voice of the Holy Spirit telling him to walk out of the front gate of the prison. So, he did. It was as if he was invisible to the guards.

He says in the book, "I didn't suffer for Jesus in prison. No! I was with Jesus and I experienced His very real presence, joy, and peace every day. It's not those in prison for the sake of the gospel who suffer. The person who suffers is he who never experiences God's intimate presence."[2] Bro. Yun found something greater to live for than what he was going to have for dinner.

CONQUERING HUNGER

Paul said, "I have learned to be satisfied with whatever I have. I know what it means to lack and I know what it means to experience overwhelming abundance. For I am trained in the secret of overcoming all things, whether in fullness or in hunger. And I find the strength of Christ's explosive power infuses me to conquer every difficulty."[3]

I have a huge difficulty with hunger and fullness. Do I really believe God can conquer that difficulty? There were many times I lost over 100 pounds. I would greatly restrict myself for a season. I'd go on a diet and I would live in hunger and deprivation.

Being hungry is not a death sentence, though. It's actually my body telling me to eat or drink a little. It doesn't have to be a lot. It should be something I have already planned so I don't allow the hunger to overwhelm me and send me on a binge.

Even if hunger does become overwhelming, such as being caught traveling without protein bars or something I can eat, I just hand my hunger to God. It's OK. I have reserves. I will eventually get to a place where there is food.

Being full is also a good feeling, a feeling of completeness. However, stuffed denotes gluttony. The children of Israel wanted to feel full. Instead they wound up overdoing it and gorging on the quail they had begged God to send them.

They were tired of manna and started complaining. "'Oh, for some meat,' they exclaimed. 'We remember the fish we used to eat for free in Egypt. And we had all the cucumbers, melons, leeks, onions and garlic we wanted. But now our appetites are gone. All we ever see is this manna!'"[4]

> Instead of being content and thankful, they acted like ravenous wolves.

Moses talked to God about the people's complaints. Among other things, God told Moses that He would give the entire group, which was estimated at 60,000 men plus women and children, meat for an entire month. Moses even doubted how God would provide, knowing that even if they butchered all their flocks and herds it wouldn't be enough.

God answered, "Has My arm lost its power? Now you will see whether or not My word comes true."[5] Then, God sent quail the people whined for. Tons of it. Instead of being content and thankful they acted like ravenous wolves.

"Now the Lord sent a wind that brought quail from the sea and let them fall all around the camp. For miles in every direction there were quail flying three feet above the ground. So the people went out and caught quail all that day and throughout the night and all the next day, too. No one gathered less than 50 bushels! They spread the quail all around the camp to dry.

"But while they were gorging themselves on the meat—while it was still in their mouths—the anger of the Lord blazed against the people, and He struck them with a severe plague. So that place was called Kibroth-hattaavah (which means 'graves of gluttony') because there they buried the people who had craved meat from Egypt."[6]

GLUTTONY

Why was God angry with them? First of all, they were not thanking God for His provision. They were doing the same thing with the quail they tried to do with manna, gathering it and saving it. They were greedy, but more than that, they weren't trusting God for tomorrow's provision.

They were not content with just having meat, they had to stuff it in their mouths. They overindulged. They were gluttonous. They did not need that much food. They were eating to the point of extravagance and waste.

"They did not believe in God or trust in His deliverance ... He rained meat down on them like dust, birds like sand on the seashore. He made them come down inside their camp, all around their tents. They ate till they were gorged—He had given them what they craved. But before they turned from what they craved, even while the food was still in their mouths, God's anger rose against them; He put to death the sturdiest among them, cutting down the young men of Israel. In spite of all this, they kept on sinning."[7]

They were eating like there would be no tomorrow. They were eating because the meat was there and they wanted it more than anything else. They did not trust God.

The Bible has strong things to say about the sin of gluttony, which is engaging in eating more physical food than one person needs. Remember when Mom would say, "Eat all your food. There are starving children in Africa"? I don't think it was because she was going to mail what we didn't eat to a third world country. She was being globally conscious and probably didn't even realize it.

If there is a certain amount of food for the entire world and we each eat only what our portion is

Gluttony is habitual greed or excess in eating.

and no more or no less, then everyone will have enough. Not too much, but enough. Instead, we are either extremely wasteful or extremely greedy. God calls greediness, gluttony. Even the dictionary calls gluttony "habitual greed or excess in eating."

Here are a few things the Bible says about gluttony. "And put a knife to your throat if you are given to gluttony."[8] "Do not join those who drink too much wine or gorge themselves on meat, for drunkards and gluttons become poor, and drowsiness clothes them in rags."[9]

In Galatians 5:19-21, which lists the sins of the flesh, The Weymouth New Testament translates the word orgies to "riotous feasting." It comes right after the word drunkenness. Overindulgence in both food and alcohol consumption is considered gluttony. "Those who live like this will not inherit the kingdom of God."[10]

Consider this rather obscure Scripture, listed among the statutes and ordinances God gave Moses for the children of Israel. This was not recounting an incident that actually happened, but it was saying if this did happen then this was what they should do. If parents brought to the elders a stubborn and rebellious son who was "a glutton and a drunkard"[11] then the elders were to gather all the men and stone him to death in order "to purge the evil from among you."[12]

WHAT'S THE BIG DEAL?

Why did God make such a big deal out of gluttony?. God wanted to be sure this tendency was purged from His people.

This was the same issue Jesus talked about only He used it in more general terms of our own selfish interests. "If anyone wishes to follow Me as My disciple, he must deny himself, set aside selfish interests, and take up his cross daily, expressing a willingness to endure whatever may come, and follow Me, believing in Me, conforming to My example in living and, if need be, suffering or perhaps dying because of faith in Me."[13]

I cannot follow Jesus and focus on myself at the same time.

I totally understand what Jesus was saying here and it hits me hard. I cannot follow Jesus and focus on myself at the same time. In essence, any addiction boils down to focusing on myself above everything else.

An addiction starts out being what gives me pleasure. I don't take into account the cost to myself or those who love me. I don't think about the future. I only think about feeling good or getting what I want for the moment I am in.

Overindulging in anything leads to dependency on it. It becomes a habit, a problem and then, a full-blown addiction. When I am addicted to something that means I am dependent on it. I obtain it at any cost. I deny myself nothing.

I am serving another master. Jesus said it best. "No one can serve two masters; for either he will hate the one and love the other, or he will be devoted to the one and despise the other. You cannot serve God and mammon, which is money, possessions, fame, status, or whatever is valued more than the Lord."[14]

It is the same as giving over control to something else. I'm grateful we are living in the age of grace, rather than the law, or I would certainly have had a sentence of stoning.

We no longer live under the laws and rules given in the Old Testament, but likewise, I was not living in the grace and freedom given to me by Christ. I had submitted myself to another master and its name was sugar.

> When I am addicted to something, I deny myself nothing.

I was not living out the admonition Paul gave. "All things are lawful for me, but not all things are profitable. All things are lawful for me, but I will not be mastered by anything."[15]

For years I thought I put God first, but looking back I can see how blind I was to what He had been trying to show me. When I finally surrendered to God the foods I craved constantly, things began to change in my life and I lost over 260 pounds in the process. Still, though, I had been like the complaining children of Israel.

When the child of Israel had been in the desert less than 90 days, they complained that they should have just stayed in

Egypt where they had food.[16] Of course, they were remembering things better than they actually had them, but still they wanted something different to eat.

God hadn't led them that far to leave them so He spoke to Moses and told Him that He would "rain down bread from heaven. The people are to go out each day and gather enough for that day. In this way, I will test them and see whether they will follow My instructions. On the sixth day they are to prepare what they bring in, and that is to be twice as much as they gather on the other days."[17]

It was a simple plan. How could they mess it up?

It was a simple plan. How could they mess it up? Moses explained the plan, but some of the people were stubborn and ignored him. They kept some of the manna for the next morning. It became bug-infested. Moses found out because it smelled. He was angry with them because of their lack of trust in God.

They soon learned that each day God provided exactly what they needed. On the day before the Sabbath God told them to gather twice as much and prepare the manna. They were to keep what was left for the next day and it would not spoil.

On the Sabbath, Moses told them that no manna would fall so they should not go and try to gather it, but they should eat what they had prepared the day before.

Some of the people still went out to gather manna on the Sabbath. They found none.

"Then the Lord said to Moses, 'How long will you refuse to keep My commands and My instructions? Bear in mind that the Lord has given you the Sabbath; that is why on the sixth day He gives you bread for two days. Everyone is to stay in. No one is to go out. So the people rested on the seventh day.'"[18]

God provided manna for the Israelites for 40 years. They ate this heavenly bread until they crossed into the Promised Land.

At times they were grateful and at times they grumbled and complained. One truth, though, remained no matter what they did. The manna fell six days a week whether they gathered it or not, whether they ate it or not.

MANNA FOR THE SOUL

The same is true for us today only in a greater way. God gives us manna for our souls. If we are hungry for God, He is as close as our hearts.

We can speak to Him out loud and He hears us. We can whisper to Him in our spirits and He hears us. We can converse with Him, read His Word, sing to Him, dance before Him, sit in silence, behold the beauty of His creation and worship Him with our very lives.

He gives us Himself as our provision. He is our bread of life and our fountain of living water.

We don't have to worry about getting enough or too much, we only need to come to the fountain and ask that He fill us to overflowing.

We must long for the sincere milk of the Word of God. We must eat of the Bread of Life. We must chew on the meat of His Word and realize that "when God fulfills our longings, sweetness fills our souls."[19]

APPLICATION

These days I'm understanding some truths for my life. These are basics many feel are a given, but for me they are truths I must hang on to with everything that is within me.

I don't have to have my stomach full all the time to be happy.

Hunger and fullness are a part of the cycle of physical nourishment.

Not everything I call hunger is physical hunger.

I don't need as much physical food as I used to, but I need more spiritual food.

> God must be first in my life. Nothing else can even come close. He is my manna

God must be first in my life. Nothing else can even come close.

I can do all things if I am tapped into the "strength of God's explosive power which infuses me to conquer every difficulty."[20]

God Himself is my manna.

Questions

1. What is hunger? How do you know if you are hungry? Do you know if it is physical hunger or emotional hunger? How can you tell the difference?

   _____

   _____

   _____

2. Why was food unimportant to Bro. Yun? Are certain foods too important to you? How would you like those feelings to change?

   _____

   _____

   _____

3. Read Phil. 4:11-13 TPT. Which do you have more trouble with hunger or fullness? How does Christ's explosive power help you conquer those difficulties?

   _____

   _____

   _____

4. In what ways have you been like the Children of Israel?

   _____

   _____

   _____

5. What is gluttony? Write your own definition and how it affects you.

   _____

   _____

   _____

6. Read Matthew 6:24 AMP and 1 Cor. 6:12 NASB. What masters are you really serving? Defend your answer.

   _____

   _____

   _____

7. What is God's daily provision for you?

   _____

   _____

   _____

Activity

SCRIPTURE: "After He had sent the crowds away, He went up on the mountain by Himself to pray; and when it was evening, He was there alone." —Matthew 14:23 NASB

SUPPLIES: Pen.

CREATIVE QUIET TIME: Many people try to fit themselves in a box when they engage in what is termed a "quiet time." Many try reading Scripture for a certain amount of time and praying. This is a great habit to get into. There are other spiritual habits as well.

Put a check beside those you currently engage in regularly and want to continue doing. Circle those you think you would enjoy or that you want to try. Note: There are additional ways on the next page.

For the next six days, I challenge you to have a creative quiet time. There are many ways to connect to Him. The list on the next page is not exhaustive. Just choose some different way to connect to God in order to infuse new energy into your time with Him.

Write about what you did each day in the space provided. There is no right or wrong way to come to God. The important thing is that we begin to find ourselves more and more hungry for Him every day.

WAYS TO CONNECT WITH GOD

Read the Bible in a year	Open Bible to random page
Study books of the Bible	Reading prophecies
Journal	Listen to a podcast/audiobook
Draw or Paint	Meditation
Forgiveness	Solitude/Silence
Inner healing	Devotional book
Keep a Sabbath time	Clear Mind of Noise
Write poetry	Quiet walks in nature
Sing	Meditate on Scripture
Dance	Acts of Service
Create a craft	Prayer/Intercession
Quiet time	Create a dream board
Memorizing Scripture	Pray the names of God
Listen to worship music	Fast
Facedown prayer	Repentance/Confession
Write short stories	Make a collage
Read a Christian book	Repeat Promises/Prophecies
Repeating His Promises	Surrender

More Inspiration

Choose a passage of Scripture. Read until something really inspires you. Stop and write a poem or draw a picture that shares the feelings or insights you got from reading.

Creative Quiet Time Chart

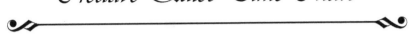

Write about how you spent each day infusing new energy into your relationship with God.

DAY 1

_____

_____

_____

_____

_____

_____

_____

_____

_____

_____

_____

DAY 2

_____

_____

_____

_____

_____

_____

_____

_____

_____

_____

_____

_____

_____

_____

_____

DAY 3

_____

_____

_____

_____

_____

_____

_____

_____

_____

_____

_____

_____

_____

_____

_____

DAY 4

_____

_____

_____

_____

_____

_____

_____

_____

_____

_____

_____

_____

_____

_____

_____

_____

DAY 5

_____

_____

_____

_____

_____

_____

_____

_____

_____

_____

_____

_____

_____

_____

_____

DAY 6

_____

_____

_____

_____

_____

_____

_____

_____

_____

_____

_____

_____

_____

_____

_____

_____

_____

ENDNOTES

1. Orr, James, M.A., D.D. General Editor. "Entry for 'HUNGER'". "International Standard Bible Encyclopedia". 1915.

2. Yun, and Paul Hattaway. The Heavenly Man: The Remarkable True Story of Chinese Christian Brother Yun. London: Monarch, 2002. Print.

3. Philippians 4:11-13 TPT

4. Numbers 11:4-6 NLT

5. Numbers 11:23 NLT

6. Numbers 11:31-35 NLT

7. Psalm 78:22, 27-32 NIV

8. Proverbs 23:2 NIV

9. Proverbs 23:20-21 NIV

10. Galatians 5:21 NIV

11. Deuteronomy 21:20 NIV

12. Deuteronomy 21:21 NIV

13. Luke 9:23 AMP

14. Matthew 6:24 AMP

15. 1 Corinthians 6:12 NASB

16. Exodus 16:3 NIV

17. Exodus 16:4-5 NIV

18. Exodus 16: 28-30 NIV

19. Proverbs 13:19 TPT

20. Philippians 4:13 TPT

Gaining the World

I muse. I wonder. I think.
is push and pull all there is,
as farther into despair I sink,
falling through the darkness I create?

I cry. I plead. I shout.
I hate this nothingness.
I need purpose. I want out
of the daily grab for more.

I stop. I sit. I ponder.
What is this life worth?
Is it to mindlessly wander?
Or is there purpose beyond my mess?

I stand. I jump. I dance.
There is more, this I know,
more than striving, more than stance.
True abundance is what I crave.

I know. I submit. I repent.
I gain by giving my life away
to the One who won't relent.
I surrender all to Him.

CHAPTER 3

GIVING UP EVERYTHING FOR FOOD

There have been times I felt like I was so hungry I thought I would die. I mean really, really hungry, like triple bacon cheeseburger, French fries, onion rings, chicken nuggets, brownies and ice cream hungry. On autopilot I'd find myself at the fast food drive-thru ordering twice as much as I had even imagined before pulling in and all at the same time vowing I would never do such a thing again.

Our appetites can involve every part of us not just our bodies, but our minds, emotions and definitely, our wills. If we feel the least bit empty in any part of our beings, our desires can overwhelm us and wipe out every commitment we just made never to overeat again.

When we feel an overwhelming void in our lives we would probably even take candy from a baby. Sometimes it just seems there is no way to placate our wants, but to eat and eat a lot. It doesn't really matter if it is spiritual, emotional or physical hunger, it is still hunger and hunger is bad and must be assuaged at any cost, or so we think.

I'M STARVING

This was a big problem for Esau. I can just see him now. Jacob and Esau were probably teenagers during the time frame of the Biblical story. Esau, the better hunter, the hairy, loud guy came in from a day of trudging through the woods not finding any game.[1]

"I'm starving!"[2] He announced to his brother, Jacob. Jacob was the quiet one whose brain was always churning.

He liked to stay around the family tents and cook. The day this incident took place, he happened to be cooking a big batch of red bean stew. It was the kind of food they cooked when they didn't have any meat. Still, the smell and thoughts of eating his brother's cooking, flavored just right, drove him crazy with hunger.

Esau didn't want to call attention to the fact he, the skilled hunter, hadn't brought back any game, so he demanded some food from his younger brother.

Jacob didn't argue. He was shrewd, though. He wasn't giving his twin brother something for nothing. "No problem. I'll give you some stew, but you have to give me something as well," Jacob countered.

Esau was hungry and when he got hungry, he got mad. "Give me some food or you'll regret it." Esau rose to his full height, blowing his words through his nose.

"Like I said, no problem." Jacob said still guarding the food. "Give me your right of the first born to the inheritance."[3]

This was a big deal. Esau was the older twin by only seconds. That meant he got the right of the firstborn, which was a double portion of what his very wealthy father owned. It included a substantial amount of land, possessions and money.

At this point, Esau didn't care about anything. He was so hungry he thought he was dying of starvation. He agreed without even thinking. His belly was governing his response. "Ok. What good is my birthright to me now if I die of hunger?"[4]

Jacob persisted and didn't give him the stew until he swore an oath. This was the same as selling all his rights as firstborn to his brother. When Esau swore the oath, the balance of power between the brothers shifted. It was a shift Esau didn't feel at the time. However, Jacob did. He didn't speak again. No words were necessary. He just dished up the stew and handed him some bread. Both brothers got what they wanted.

Esau was no longer hungry and in the moment that was all that mattered.

Esau ate and left. To Esau, life didn't change that day except that his belly was full for the moment. The oath-swearing thing was no big deal. He had what he wanted. He was no longer hungry and that was all that mattered.

Esau, "showed contempt for his rights as the firstborn"[5] by doing this. Perhaps he wasn't too concerned because in their culture there were two gifts the father could bestow, the birthright and the blessing. Jacob now had the birthright, but Esau knew he was his father's favorite. Surely he'd get the blessing.

I doubt Esau thought about much besides satisfying his appetite. It doesn't say at this point that Esau even had a thought of, "Man, I just gave away my inheritance." His desires had ruled him from the very beginning.

This is born out through a New Testament passage that carries a warning to future generations, "See that no one is sexually immoral, or is godless like Esau, who for a single meal sold his inheritance rights as the oldest son. Afterward, as you know, when he wanted to inherit this blessing, he was rejected. Even though he sought the blessing with tears, he could not change what he had done."[6] It wasn't his father who rejected him, though. His father had no control over the situation. It was God Himself who allowed the natural consequences to play out.

LIKE FATHER, LIKE SON

Scripture says the reason Issac, the boys' father, loved Esau was because of the wild game he brought home.[7] Both Esau and his father were ruled by their appetites.

Isaac continued to grow his wealth and by chapter 27, he had become old and blind. One big thing hadn't changed, though. He still lived to eat the meat that Esau brought him.

The New American Commentary goes so far as to say, "Isaac's pleasure in eating game distracted him, contributing to his negligence."[8]

He said to Esau, "Take your bow and a quiver full of arrows and go out into the open country and hunt some wild game for me. Prepare my favorite dish and bring it here for me to eat. Then I will pronounce the blessing that belongs to you, my firstborn son, before I die."[9]

This failed because Rebekah, the boys' mother who favored Jacob, heard the conversation and instead had Jacob bring her two goats from their flock. She prepared them and had Jacob take them to his father. Jacob put on Esau's clothes and covered his arms and neck with the goatskin in order to trick Isaac into giving him the blessing instead of Esau.

> He satisfied his appetite before giving the blessing.

In the end, the ruse worked and Jacob got the father's blessing. Jacob already had the birthright, which was the majority of his father's possessions. By deception, he also received his father's blessing, which was a prophecy of what he would become in life.

It's notable that Isaac ate his dinner and drank his wine before kissing his son. In other words, he satisfied his appetite before giving the blessing. Then, when he smelled the clothes of Esau and believed it to be Esau, he bestowed an irrevocable blessing on Jacob, the younger son.

He essentially blessed him with everything in heaven, on earth, grain, new wine, nations falling at his feet and that he would be lord over his brothers. Finally, he said, "All who curse you will be cursed and all who bless you will be blessed."[10]

It was an all-encompassing blessing meant to give Esau everything and Jacob nothing. Instead the reverse happened.

The only blessing left for Isaac to give Esau was that he would serve his brother.[11]

Jacob and his mother clearly tricked Esau and Issac. Both Esau and Isaac had more interest in the foods they were eating than the birthright or blessing. We know from the Hebrews passage that in the end when Esau realized what he had done in selling his birthright for a bowl of stew he was sad and tried to get it back, but God took the swearing of the oath very seriously.[12] What had been done could not be undone.

Isaac was more aware of the power of the blessing than Esau, but he still ate first and after he was satisfied with the meal, blessed the wrong son. Rebekah knew her husband would be less inclined to wonder about who had fed him if the meal was beyond satisfying. She knew her husband's appetite.

ESAU'S CHANGE

Esau was ready to kill Jacob after he stole the blessing. Jacob left and was gone for many years. When he decided to return to his homeland and make amends with Esau, both brothers were changed men.

Jacob approached his brother, who had 400 men with him. Jacob bowed to the ground seven times as he approached Esau. The change in Esau can be seen because he ran to Jacob, embraced him, threw his arms around his neck, kissed him and together they wept.[13]

Esau was no longer a man bent on revenge. He had settled in as one who was in charge of many and secure in his position. The entire tone of the meeting indicated that Esau's appetite had been conquered along the way. The anger had vanished.

How did he conquer his fleshly desires? We do not know for sure. We do know this, Esau was a burly, loud hunter who became a loving brother. How did that happen? This kind of change could only happen if Esau had totally surrendered to God.

APPLICATION

There have been times in my life when, even though I weighed over 400 pounds, I thought I'd die if I didn't have something to eat. Not just anything to eat, though. It had to be something sweet or starchy with lots of carbohydrates to give me energy. At least that's what I told myself and what I thought.

The truth was I didn't need anything to eat. My body was just being taken over by my stomach. I had trained my body to listen to the wrong part of me. Many times I wasn't "famished" like Esau. I hadn't gone all day without food. I just had an insatiable appetite.

Part of it had to do with being afraid and not feeling protected, feeling sad and not knowing where to find real comfort and being lonely and not trusting companionship from any place, but food. Sad, but true.

I had trained my body to listen to the wrong part of me.

I didn't connect the dots that God, the Father. is the One who protects me.[14] The Holy Spirit is the Comforter[15] and the only place I can find true comfort. Jesus is my companion[16] who walks this journey with me.

I had been living as if my stomach was my god. "For, as I have often told you before and now tell you again even with tears, many live as enemies of the cross of Christ. Their destiny is destruction, their god is their stomach, and their glory is in their shame. Their mind is set on earthly things, but our citizenship is in heaven. And we eagerly await a Savior from there, the Lord Jesus Christ."[17]

Realizing this fact made me sick to think my stomach was the thing I was worshipping instead of God. I didn't like this truth, but it was larger than life. I was Esau, not concerned about anything, but my next meal. Not even caring about my future or the future of any family I might one day have. I lived in the moment. I lived for what I wanted.

The fact that I was not alone in this situation did little to relieve the guilt I felt over what I had done. I needed only to look around to find people living for what gave them pleasure. I used to love to point fingers at those who did drugs, drank alcohol, engaged in extramarital sexual activities, gambled, spent money they didn't have or engaged in pornography. The list was endless and could go on and on. Anything could be on that list as long as I was not guilty of it.

GIMME, GIMME

I, like many other Christians, even Christian leaders, don't like to talk about the sin of making our stomach our god. No, that hits too close to home. We live in a gimme, gimme world, a world that screams indulgence on every corner, but as Christians we many times indulge in the one thing we rarely talk about as sin—overeating.

What are we really trying to get when we overeat? We take our shopping list to God and expect Him to fulfill our every want while as many as one out of every nine people are starving. We call presenting our "I want" list to God—prayer. I often feel God is just shaking His head and saying, "When will they ever get it?"

What we want is all we think about. After all, we've had a long day. We deserve what we want and what we want includes everything unhealthy for us, but we will eat it because that's what we want.

I am just like Esau who gave up everything for a bowl of red bean stew. He even gave his identity. From that day on he was called, "Red" because of the red bean stew.[18] From then on, every time someone said, "Hey Red," he was reminded that he had allowed his appetite to take away one of the things that mattered most in his life, not only his inheritance, but the blessing as well.

> It will be forever remembered that Israel serves the God of Abraham, Isaac and Jacob, not Esau.

God does not leave him destitute though. He is blessed, but we see by the final meeting of Jacob and Esau that Jacob is more blessed. He shares gifts with Esau, but has no need of the gifts Esau offers him.[19]

Down through the annals of time it will forever be remembered that Israel serves the God of Abraham, Issac and Jacob,[20] not Esau.

Questions:

1. In what ways do you make your appetite or your stomach your god instead of God? In other words, in what ways do you rely on substances, activities, interests, relationships or other things more than God?

_____

_____

_____

2. Do you think Esau's appetite was ever conquered? How might that have happened? Defend your answer.

_____

_____

_____

3. What does it mean when we talk about God being the God of Abraham, Isaac and Jacob, but not Esau? Esau was the first-born. What more did he give up because of his appetite besides wealth?

_____

_____

_____

4. What appetites do you have that need to be conquered? These might not be food. They might be other fleshly desires or wants you have allowed to rule your life. List these. Be specific.

_____

_____

_____

5. Many times we hide behind our addictions thinking they provide us protection of some sort. How can we allow God to be our protector instead of the substances we crave? What are some tangible things we can do?

_____

_____

_____

_____

6. How does the Holy Spirit provide us comfort? Why do we think food or other things are more comforting to us than Him?

_____

_____

_____

_____

7. How can you practice allowing the Holy Spirit to be your Source? List all the ways you can think of.

_____

_____

_____

_____

_____

8. Certain foods or other wants sometimes become like trusted friends and companions. How have you allowed this to happen? How has this affected your life?

_____

_____

_____

_____

9. How can you allow Jesus to be your companion and guide on your journey rather than substances?

_____

_____

_____

_____

Activity

SCRIPTURE: "And He was saying to them all, "If anyone wishes to follow Me, as My disciple, he must deny himself, set aside selfish interests, and take up his cross daily, expressing a willingness to endure whatever may come, and follow Me, believing in Me, conforming to My example in living and, if need be, suffering or perhaps dying because of faith in Me." —Luke 9:23 AMP

SUPPLIES: small sticky notes, colored markers or pens, a method to play music and a copy of "Oceans" or "I Surrender" by Hillsong.

SELFISH DESIRES: Visual representatives and reminders are always good. In the space provided on the next page or pages, draw pictures or simply write words to represent the things you are running to (your selfish desires) instead of to God. These might include substances, activities, interests, relationships or other things. You might choose to color these in denoting the colors they make you feel, make them bigger or smaller depending on how you view their place in your life. Make the words depict how you feel about these things in your life.

List the foods, drinks, drugs and activities that take your focus from God. List hobbies or other interests that eat up your time, relationships that might be difficult or damaging and any other things that are taking over your life. The more specific you can be the better.

When you are finished, spend some time in prayer. Think about the ways you have put each of these in place of God. Ask God to show you how He can fill that void more than the things you have listed.

When you are ready, hand each thing on your paper to God. Tell Him, "I no longer want to put this in the place of You, God. I hand it to You. Show me how to put You in the number one position in my life instead of this thing. Please give me a gift to aid me in completely surrendering this."

Using sticky notes write what God gives you in exchange for that item on your list. Place the sticky note with the gift He gave you over the item you handed to Him. Things He has given me are comfort, love, peace, grace, patience, joy, mercy, kindness, faith, glory, His presence, gentleness, His heart, strength, goodness, courage and self-control. There are many other things as well. Don't demand that He give You a gift. Just receive and be open to receiving.

When you have finished, play a song of surrender ("I Surrender" or "Oceans" by Hillsong). Pray a prayer of surrender to God regarding the things you have been going to instead of to Him. Let your surrender song be a reminder of this time.

Selfish Desires Chart

More Inspiration

Cut a piece of typing paper into small squares or strips. On each piece of paper write one thing that is a selfish desire you want to get rid of. As you hand each of these to God, tear the piece of paper into tiny shreds over a trash can. It is now gone! Ask God, what do you give me in exchange? Write the things He gives you here.

ENDNOTES

1. Genesis 25:27-34 NLT

2. Genesis 25:30 NLT

3. Genesis 25:31 NLT

4. Genesis 25:32 NLT

5. Genesis 25:34 NLT

6. Hebrews 12:16-17 NIV

7. Genesis 25:28 NLT

8. Clendenen, E. Ray. The New American Commentary: An Exegetical and Theological Exposition of Holy Scripture: NIV Text. Nashville, TN: Broadman & Holman, 1991. Print.

9. Genesis 27:3-4 NLT

10. Genesis 27:29 NLT

11. Genesis 27:40 NLT

12. Hebrews 12:16-17 NIV

13. Genesis 33:3-5 NLT

14. Isaiah 41:10 NLT

15. John 14:26 KJV

16. John 15:12-14 NKJV

17. Philippians 3:18-20 NIV

18. Genesis 25:30 NLT

19. Genesis 33:11, 15 NLT

20. Acts 3:13 NLT

Distractions and Grace

Distractions. They call to me from everywhere.
I want to be God's, yet I am focused just on me.

They pull me towards another goal,
towards what I want, towards a god of my making.

Ah, but God. I know His presence
will fulfill my every need. It is my choice.

Instead, I run to distractions, which fast
become addictions, strongholds that hold me tight.

I see that I am bound, but I want to be free.
I cry out to Him and He hears me still.

Morning dawns. The new has come.
The old has to go to make way for
Him to be my all-in-all.

Distractions still arise, but I have God's promises
in place. I look to Him and Him alone.

His sweet grace fulfills my every need.
I surrender who I am to Him and He is enough.

SWEET HUNGER

CHAPTER 4

WHY DID
I EAT THAT?

blame it on the noise of life. There's frustration at every turn, loud music, kids screaming, echoes blaring, whistles tweeting and water rushing. It's enough to make me want to eat something decadent.

I've just entered the indoor community pool where I go to walk in the water at least five days a week. The problem is, it's a school holiday. It's late afternoon and every kid in the world has come here. I hate to exercise in the water and dodge children at the same time.

On top of all of that just as I walked into the pool area, I got a business call I'd been waiting for all day. There is no place to take a phone call once I am in my bathing suit and in the cavernous, echo-ridden pool area. How can I tell a rather important person that I can't talk now even though I've been waiting for the call all day?

It's enough to make a food addict want to cave. It's the noise of life I blame for this feeling that if I could just eat something everything would be so much better.

As I thought about this tempting pull one name popped into my head—Eve. I asked myself, was it the noise of life that caused Eve to eat the forbidden fruit? I knew, though, if Eve and everyone down through the ages until me had resisted and hadn't eaten, I would have. I'm very sure of it. There has never been a bigger food addict than me. I'm sure my temptation tree would have cinnamon crunch bagels hanging on it.

NOISE WITHIN

Where did Eve's noise come from? She lived in a paradise fashioned by the Creator just for her and Adam. There were no other people. There were animals over which they had authority. There was food provided for them. There was a lush and beautiful land.

They had fellowship with the God of the universe. He walked with them. He communicated with them. They knew what He said. They didn't have to question if He said it. It was clear. They felt the glory of His close presence. This was the way it was supposed to be. This was God's plan.

This was the way it was supposed to be. This was God's plan.

A big part of this plan was that Adam and Eve, as the first man and woman, could choose this lifestyle. If they made the obviously correct choice, they could eat from the tree of life forever. That meant they would never taste of death, decay and disease. Their union with God would be unending.

He also gave the angels free will. It didn't go so well for some of the angels. Satan was once known as the angel of light.

He rebelled against God and was cast from heaven along with a myriad of other angels.[1]

We blame a lot of what happened in the garden on the serpent. He plays a major role to be sure, but I don't think he is the major source of noise for Eve. I believe her noise came from within and Satan picked up on it because he recognized the signs. He was the one who wanted to be like God.[2]

As we know from the story in Genesis, God told Adam he could eat freely from any tree in the garden except the tree of the knowledge of blessing and calamity.[3] Just to make sure they were not confused about what the right choice was, God told Adam that if he did eat from this tree he would die.[4] Adam had no concept of death. He had not seen death, but he knew the tree of life excluded him from death. Death was no serious threat to Adam. Inside his head he said, "Life is good. I'm going to live forever."

TEMPTATION

Eve knew God's command not to eat from this tree. She answered Satan's question with what God had told Adam.[5] Here is where I recognized that Eve had a lot of noise in her head. She had been wondering about this seemingly ridiculous command of God. She wondered why she and Adam had to stay away from this one tree. What was special about it? Was the fruit exclusively for God? Was it so delicious He wanted to keep it only for Himself?

Satan spoke to the questions that were bothering her. He couldn't read her mind, but he could put himself in her place. He had been there once. He wanted to be like God. He used that desire to stir up the noise he surmised was already building in her.

He told her she wouldn't die, which contradicted what God said. "God knows that your eyes will be opened as soon as you eat it. Then you will be like God, knowing both good and evil."[6] The noise was at a crescendo now. She wanted to be God-like. She wanted to be in control.

CONTROL

OK, I get that part. I've been a controller and I know many others who are as well. I'm trying to give control away these days, but I've controlled so well no one wants to take it off my hands. It's a tangled web I've woven, but I am getting out as I find people to hand things off to. Eve was about to find out how messy wanting to be like God could get.

Eve's brain couldn't comprehend why God would let her and Adam be in control of everything in the garden, but would keep this one prize from them. After all, they had a big job to do. They needed the special delicacy this tree provided.

The fruit looks like whatever is our biggest temptation.

The fruit looks like whatever is our biggest temptation, whether it be food, alcohol, drugs, pornography, more and more things, better job, bigger house or a different spouse. And it seems totally irresistible close up.

Until that moment of temptation, Eve had never been that close to what God told her not to touch. She'd never breathed in its delectable aroma. She'd never seen the beauty of its appearance. She licked her lips. She knew the taste was something incredible—the delicacy of God, the one with all power, knowledge and wisdom.

It was the one thing in the garden she was told she couldn't have. It was the one thing she had to have.

Adam was there for the whole thing. His internal noise might have been something like, "I have to eat it because if I don't she is going to be like God and then where does that leave me?"

She ate it and he ate it and that was that. Satan was right about one thing. They didn't die, at least not right away.[7]

Adam and Eve immediately realized they were naked and so they hid from God. I can really relate to this. There have been times I have eaten bags of candy while sitting in my room watching television. I assumed since I could see no one else in the room, no one, not even God, knew what I was doing.

> It was the one thing in the garden she was told she couldn't have. It was the one thing she had to have.

It was a false assurance because of course, God knows everything, sees everything even before I do it. I stand unmasked, naked before Him. He knows every part of me. I cannot hide.

If Adam and Eve didn't know that before they ate from the forbidden tree, they knew it once they disobeyed. They heard Him walking in the garden in the cool of the evening and hid themselves from His presence.[8] God asked Adam a simple question, "Where are you?" He asked Adam the question in order to hear his answer. God already knew the answer. Why did He ask the question if He already knew the answer?

I remember a time after God had dealt with me about my addiction to processed sugar and gluten. I went to a conference and I ate a cookie. I hadn't eaten a cookie in over a year. It tasted so good that I had to have another and another. Then I took some home supposedly for my husband, who might eat one cookie a month, seriously.

When God asks me a question, it's not because He doesn't know the answer. He wants me to think.

On the way home in the quiet of the car driving along a dark highway, God asked me a question: "What are you doing?" It's not that the omniscient God didn't know the answer. He was not seeking to add information to His databank. He wanted to make me think.

I said, "I'm throwing this cookie out the window," and I did. I got home and handed the rest of the cookies over to my husband and told him to hide them from me. I never saw them again and I never wanted to.

Adam answered God's question in a strange sort of way. He didn't immediately say, "I ate what you told me not to eat." He said, "I heard the sound of You in the garden and I was afraid because I was naked; so I hid myself."[9]

Interesting answer, but God knew the deeper truth and asked, "Who told you that you were naked?"[10] Up to this point they were so innocent they had no need to cover themselves. Now that they had the knowledge about what happened when evil entered their lives, they realized they had to cover themselves. Then, God added, "Have you eaten from the tree of which I commanded you not to eat?"[11]

Adam tried to take no blame in the situation. He said, "The woman whom You gave to be with me, she gave me from the tree and I ate."[12]

WHY WOULD YOU EAT THAT?

When God addressed Eve He said, "Why on earth would you eat that?" OK, that's my paraphrase. He really asked, "What have you done?"[13] Since she knew by now that she was in big trouble, she took the only road open to her. She blamed the serpent for deceiving her.

This was a sad day for the world. God gave the proclamation of what would befall all of humanity because of Adam and Eve's rebellion. He told them that their lives were going to be full of calamity and hard work. The blessings they had had would cease.[14]

God banished Adam and Eve from Paradise and set a cherubim with a flaming sword to guard the entrance.[15] No more would mankind be able to eat of the tree of life. God did this for one reason and one reason only. He did it out of love. He knew what a tragedy it would be for mankind to live forever in a fallen state never again to have the possibility of access to God or eternal life.

This was a sad day for the world.

God's warning was true. By eating of the tree of the knowledge of good and evil, Adam and Eve ushered death into the world. It was death not only for themselves, but for all mankind. Their future did not look bright.

God knew mankind would fall. He prepared for it before time began. He gave us free will so we have a choice. We can choose to love Him. We are not and never have been forced to love Him. Control is not love.

I've heard mothers tell their children, "You have to obey me. I'm your mother." I never wanted my children to feel obligated to obey me. I wanted them to obey me because they chose to love me and, therefore, obey out of that love.

ANOTHER ADAM

God feels the same way about us. Eve messed up. Adam messed up. God, though, provided another Adam[16] (Jesus), who made a way for the first Adam (all of us) to make a better choice. To choose Christ is to choose God, to choose to love.

It's also about following God's ways and His commands towards purpose and mission while we are here on earth.

God gave Adam and Eve a command to be fruitful and multiply. They carried out His command bearing children even after their son Cain killed his brother, Abel. They messed up, but their ongoing obedience to that command proved they had repented and stayed true to God. They understood what they had and what they had lost.

Who could forget the glory of God? Adam and Eve never forgot. Yet they lived on doing everything they knew to do to worship and reverently serve God.

It would be eons before Christ, as the second Adam, came on the scene. "For since death came through a man, the resurrection of the dead comes also through a man. For as in Adam all die, so in Christ all will be made alive."[17]

APPLICATION

We might have had a life of ease if Eve hadn't listened to the tempter stirring up the noises inside her head. However, we know one thing for certain, if we listen to the noises outside and inside our heads, we will not hear the voice of our Creator, who gently calls to us to come closer.

On occasions, I have tasted of the glory of God. For me, it usually comes as my face is on the floor crying out for His presence and guidance in my life or sitting in solitude and silence making space and time to just be with Him. I feel a blanketing presence of the Lord so strong I dare not look up lest His presence slay me. When the glory leaves, there is a void that only time with Him can fill again. And I long for morning to come when I can steal away with Him again.

> He gently calls us to come closer.

I want to ask Eve, "Why would you eat that? You had all of Him, His very presence to walk with you, to engage in conversation. Why would you?"

I can't blame Eve, though, I sometimes do the same thing myself. His presence is with me always, but I don't always seek His glory that rests in moments of clarity.

That kind of presence only comes when I surrender totally to Him, when I am willing to confess and repent of every ounce of failure or when I openly lay myself on the altar and ask that He show me the other areas that need to be touched. Then, it is crystal clear. I rise and follow Him in obedience.

DISOBEDIENCE AND HEARING GOD

My disobedience shuts off hearing and experiencing the presence of God in my life. For me, disobedience comes mainly in the form of eating what I know God has clearly told me not to eat. Of course, there are other types of disobedience. Whatever form it takes, it is still disobedience. No one type of disobedience is worse than another.

> My disobedience shuts off hearing and experiencing the presence of God in my life.

Many times, though, we assume that one bite of a piece of cake is not a big deal. It's not like I killed someone. However, God has clearly told me not to eat things made with sugar and flour because they are very addictive to me. For me to do that is disobedience to God. That is the definition of sin.

"Why would you eat that?" is a question that looms large in my mind when I even think about being disobedient to what God has shown me to do. It is a question that guides me when friends I'm with mention going to the restaurant that makes cinnamon crunch bagels. I can say, "Sure we can eat there." I can do that because I choose something from the menu, like the delicious grilled chicken, pecan and strawberry salad that is OK between God and me.

When the pull of the cinnamon crunch bagels gets strong, I hear God's voice ask, "Are you going to eat that?" I say, "No, God. I am your child of obedience. I want the lasting feel of the close communion with you more than I want the taste of those things which will only last for a moment." And I know He is smiling and that means more than anything earth can provide.

"O taste and see that the Lord our God is good. How blessed, fortunate, prosperous and favored by God is the man (or woman) who takes refuge in Him."[18]

This verse guides me to obedience and straight to His side. I put aside the noise in my head and the distractions that call to me from the bakery case. I do it for one reason only. I do it for His presence in my life and nothing else.

He never moves, but when I cease to dine at His table of blessings, I move and He seems distant. I never again want to feel disconnected from Him.

Questions

1. What screams louder at you, the noise of life that surrounds you or the noise within? What specifically is the noise saying to you?

_____

_____

2. Why does Satan seem to know our hot buttons so well?

_____

_____

3. What was the noise in Eve's head? Have you ever had a similar noise in your head? What did it say to you? Be specific.

_____

_____

_____

4. Has being a controller ever been a problem with you? In what way? How can you stop having to always control every circumstance?

_____

_____

5. What is the fruit hanging on your tree? What about it is tempting?

_____

_____

6. Have you ever tried to hide from God? What was it you were hiding?

_____

_____

7. Why did God ask Adam, "Where are you" when He already knew the answer? Why might He ask you the same thing?

_____

_____

8. What shuts down hearing and experiencing the presence of God in your life?

_____

_____

9. What is the thing that tempts you and calls you to be disobedient to God? When are you most tempted?

_____

_____

10. What kind of emotions might lead you to give in to temptation? Being angry, sad, rejected, unloved, lonely, overwhelmed, frustrated or something else? Please list.

_____

_____

_____

_____

11. What could you do instead of giving in to the temptation? What would help take care of the emotions better than food or other things you are tempted to do?

_____

_____

_____

_____

12. In what ways can you invite God's presence into the time of temptation?

_____

_____

_____

_____

Activity

SCRIPTURE: "The temptations in your life are no different from what others experience. And God is faithful. He will not allow the temptation to be more than you can stand. When you are tempted, he will show you a way out so that you can endure."
—1 Corinthians 10:13 NLT

SUPPLIES: Pen, chart.

TEMPTATIONS CHART: Make a "Temptations Chart." Divide a piece of paper into three columns or use the page provided in this book. Name the columns: Emotions, Temptations, Better Solutions.

In the first column write the various emotions you have that lead you to do something you shouldn't. Emotions such as anger, loneliness, stress, sadness, afraid, ashamed, guilty, frustrated, overwhelmed, overworked. In the second column put what you normally go to when you feel that emotion. What are you tempted to eat or do that you know you shouldn't?

Different emotions will lead us to do different things. Think through this. Think back to the last time you felt that emotion and what you felt tempted to do. In the third column list a better solution than what you are tempted to do.

For instance in the first column I might write stressed. My first response to stress of any kind used to be to eat. In the second column I would put eat fast food because if I was feeling stressed and overwhelmed I would want something quick to eat so I would go through fast food and get unhealthy carbohydrate-laden foods, go for a drive and gobble them down before going home and fixing dinner for my family and eating yet again.

In the third column, think of a better solution and list that. For me I realized going for a drive, minus the fast food, was a better solution. In reality it was the going for a drive that soothed my emotions and quieted me.

Making a chart such as this is helpful to pre-plan what you can do in times of temptation. It also helps as a way of escape from that temptation. God will provide those ways of escape, but we need to have made a firm decision ahead of time that we will take God's way out of temptation.

Here's the truth. If we pray for a way we need to take it. If we pre-plan for temptation to occur,we will be better able to take the way of escape God has already shown us to take. The key to this activity is to refer back often to this chart and remember what you need to do in times of temptation.

More Inspiration

Get some colorful postcards. On the cards write scriptures that remind you to turn to God in time of temptation. You may wish to type these on the computer and glue them to the card. Memorize one a month and ask God to recall them to your mind when you need them. Make copies and post them on your refrigerator, bedroom mirror, in your car or around your office or desk.

EMOTIONS	TEMPTATIONS	BETTER SOLUTIONS
1.		
2.		
3.		
4.		
5.		
6.		
7.		

ENDNOTES

1. Luke 10:18, Rev. 12:7-9 NIV
2. Isaiah 14:12-14 NLT
3. Genesis 2:16-17 AMP
4. Genesis 2:17 NLT
5. Genesis 3:1-3 NLT
6. Genesis 3:5 NLT
7. Genesis 3:6 NLT
8. Genesis 3:8 NLT
9. Genesis 3:10 NLT
10. Genesis 3:11 NLT
11. Genesis 3:11 NLT
12. Genesis 3:12 NLT
13. Genesis 3:13 NLT
14. Genesis 3:16-19 NLT
15. Genesis 3:22-24 NLT
16. 1 Corinthians 15:45 NLT
17. 1 Corinthians 15:21-22 NLT
18. Psalm 34:8 AMP

"O taste and see that the
Lord our God is good.
How blessed, fortunate,
prosperous and favored by
God is the man or woman
who takes refuge in Him."

PSALM 34:8 AMP

SWEET HUNGER

Give Me

God, Give me this day everything I want.

Feed me each day exactly what I crave.

Heal me of every disease, even
those of my own making.

Keep me from ever experiencing trouble or turmoil.

Bless me with money to make all my wishes come true.

Help me to be successful in every
endeavor and never fail.

Save me for all of eternity, but most of all from myself.

And … make me just like Jesus.

My Child, I always meet your needs,

but I will not promise your wants.

My storehouse is open, but not for you

to take so much it harms you.

Overeating is one reason you have so many diseases.

In this world you will have trouble,

but I have overcome the world.

Blessings come when you are ready to

be good stewards of them.

Success is a matter of perspective.

Mine is very different from yours.

I have saved you for all of eternity.

You have to work on the other part.

And … you have a ways to go to be like My Son.

SWEET HUNGER

BEING FED BY THE MASTER

Growing up and even into my adult years, food was pleasure. A full stomach meant real life to me. I never wanted to be without food. Maybe it was all those pictures of starving children in Africa and Bangladesh that made me shudder. I was alive, satisfied and happy, as long as my belly was full.

It was the mindset of lack, and I know that now, but as a child I equated happiness with lots of high-calorie foods. Big family dinners were bright spots in my life. They were the times I was happiest. That should have been because of the myriad of relatives who were there, but I focused on what was for dinner.

The special food served by special people in my life made me feel loved. Food, though, would satisfy only for a moment, the one moment I was in. Then, just like any drug of choice, I needed more to get that same high feeling. This especially happened when I ate foods have sugar and high carbohydrate content. When I would start eating those types of food I couldn't stop.

It wasn't because I was physically hungry, though. It was because those types of foods reminded me of good times. Then, the more I ate them, the more they morphed into a purely selfish indulgence. Given all of this it was no wonder I had a hard time understanding being hungry for Jesus. I was too full of food to be hungry for anything else.

I don't think even the dictionary describes hunger very well. It says it is the "feeling of discomfort or weakness caused by the lack of food, coupled with the desire to eat." It also defines it as "to feel or suffer hunger through lack of no food" or to "have a strong desire or craving for".

My personal idea of hunger best fit the last one because I wasn't really feeling physically weak when I used the words, "I'm hungry." I should have said I want or I crave this food because that's what it was. I should be craving and desiring the sincere milk of the Word of God,[1] rather than something to fill my appetite.

EATING JESUS, SAY WHAT?

Jesus went one step further and told the people they shouldn't just crave God's Word, they should eat His flesh and drink His blood.

There is no doubt that Jesus was controversial when He walked on earth. It seemed that He spoke in riddles. Some felt what He was calling them to do was ridiculous and they dismissed them.

This was very true when Jesus made an astounding statement to the Jews of all people. "I am the bread of life! Your ancestors ate manna in the wilderness, but they all died. Anyone who eats the bread from heaven, however, will never die. I am the living bread that came down from heaven. Anyone who eats this bread will live forever; and this bread, which I will offer so the world may live, is My flesh."[2]

> Jesus was hiding a spiritual truth in plain sight.

Every time Jesus spoke to the people He told them eternal truths wrapped in everyday illustrations. There is nothing more everyday than eating bread. It was what they ate three times a day. He was a Jew and knew that. He was speaking their language, but they could not catch the eternal truth He was giving them.

They started arguing with each other thinking He was asking them to eat His actual flesh. Jesus was hiding a spiritual truth in plain sight. Instead of placating them and explaining what He was trying to get them to understand, He went into it even deeper.

"I tell you the truth, unless you eat the flesh of the Son of Man and drink His blood, you cannot have eternal life within you. But anyone who eats My flesh and drinks My blood has eternal life, and I will raise that person at the last day. For My flesh is true food, and my blood is true drink.

"Anyone who eats My flesh and drinks My blood remains in Me, and I in him. I live because of the living Father who sent Me; in the same way, anyone who feeds on Me will live because of Me. I am the true bread that came down from heaven. Anyone who eats this bread will not die as your ancestors did (even though they ate the manna) but will live forever."[3]

The people were thinking, "You want us to eat Your flesh and drink your blood, Jesus? What are we cannibals, werewolves, zombies?" This was really over the top for them to grasp. Imagine trying to figure out what He was saying. It could only mean the literal words, right?

ARE YOU ALL IN?

This was Jesus' way of discovering who was all in and who was not. He was saying that accepting Him as the way to live eternally is as necessary as food and drink is to live physically. He was promising an entirely new and different kind of life, one which could only be understood in the spiritual, not the natural.

Jesus was well aware the disciples considered this teaching a little over the top. Yet, the only explanation He gave them was, "It is the Spirit who gives life. The flesh profits nothing. The words that I have spoken to you are spirit and are life."[4]

Many who were following Jesus just for the things He did for them or for the food He fed them left Him that day. As the groupies dropped away, Jesus queried the 12 disciples to find out if they were also going to leave. Peter answered, "Lord, to whom shall we go? You have the words of eternal life. We have believed and have come to know that You are the Holy One of God."[5]

Peter gave the right answer, though He still may not have figured out what Jesus was really saying. It probably wouldn't be until Jesus' resurrection, ascension and the coming of the

Holy Spirit that the disciples actually understood that following Jesus is the only true path to life abundant and eternal.

This whole exchange began when a crowd of people followed Jesus "because they saw the signs which He was performing on those who were sick."[6] Jesus had gone away to be alone with His disciples. When He saw a huge crowd of people coming to Him He asked Philip, "Where are we to buy bread so that these may eat?"[7]

Jesus was about to do a miracle. He was testing Philip to see if he would come up with a limited human and very physical response, which he did. Philip answered they didn't have enough money to buy bread for everyone to even eat a little bite.

Andrew, though, offered a little boy's lunch to Jesus— five loaves and two fishes. He was swooping in like the super hero to save the day. However, Andrew's faith was as lacking as Philip's. He said, "But what are these for so many people?"[8]

The disciples were thinking about what they could see in the natural.

The multiplication of the loaves and fishes was a physical miracle. They had no power or strength in the natural to feed this crowd of people even though in Mark's gospel account of the same story, Jesus tells the disciples, "You give them something to eat."[9]

True to form, the disciples were thinking about what they could see and produce in the natural. Jesus was going to show them what can happen when the strength and power of God is applied to a seemingly impossible situation.

It's a well-known story. He had them sit down in groups, took the loaves and fish, asked God the Father to bless the food, then began breaking the bread and fish.

There is more than enough spiritual truth to satisfy us and those we meet.

"He kept giving them to the disciples to set before them. They all ate and were satisfied and picked up 12 baskets of the bread and fish."[10]

They all ate, all 5,000 men and probably as many or more women and children who were with them, and still there were plenty of leftovers to share with others the disciples met along the way. There is significance even in the leftovers.

If we see what Jesus did this day in feeding the people as having a deeper meaning that He alone is the bread of life, then the leftovers mean He has more than enough spiritual truth to satisfy us and those we meet. We only need to be hungry enough to receive it and bold enough to share it.

KING OF MY STOMACH

Because their bellies were full and they saw that Jesus had essentially made much food out of a very little, the people declared, "Surely, this is the Prophet who is to come into the world."[11] In other words, He filled their bellies. They were fat and happy and they declared Him King, at least of their stomachs.

After the people left, Jesus needed time alone so He sent the disciples on across the sea while he stole away up the mountain to pray. The next day the people came back only to find the disciples' boats gone. So they followed Jesus across the Sea of Galilee. When they found Him they sound a bit miffed when they asked, "When did You get here?"[12] It's almost like saying, "Why did You go off without us?"

Jesus saw their true intent. He said, "You seek Me not because you saw signs, but because you ate of the loaves and were filled. Do not work for the food which perishes, but for the food which endures to eternal life, which the Son of Man will give to you."[13]

This, then, started the conversation we talked about earlier. Jesus specifically told them, "I am the Bread of Life. He who comes to Me will not hunger and he who believes in Me will never thirst."[14]

Then, He gave them the Words of Life. "This is the will of My Father, that everyone who beholds the Son and believes in Him will have eternal life."[15]

The sign He was giving them was Himself. Only through Jesus could they obtain real life. He was explaining the truth that hungering and thirsting in the natural was just for a season, but hungering and thirsting for Jesus means an abundant life here and in eternity.

SELF-CENTERED INDULGENCE

There is a place for food, of course. It's supposed to be fuel for our bodies so we can be fit warriors for the Kingdom of God here on earth. However, Jesus clearly said, "If any of you wants to be My follower, you must turn from your selfish ways, take up your cross daily, and follow me."[16]

Just like anything, food can become an indulgence, which would be sin because Jesus requires us to deny our self-centered ways, take up our crosses, not just once, but daily or constantly. Still we persist in our personal desires. For me that was eating whatever I wanted, whenever I wanted.

"Food is for the stomach and the stomach is for food, but God will do away with both of them."[17] The necessity of eating is a fleeting thing that only exists here on earth. It's not something to be worshipped or sought after. We don't worship Jesus because He gives us food. We thank Him for that and for all the other blessings He provides for us, but we worship Him because He gave His life for us.

He fed the 5,000 simply to provide physical sustenance, not to be called a prophet. This miracle flowed out of what Jesus saw as a human need. However, the people did not get the significance. He was giving them a physical illustration that He is our life and sustenance. He is our everything.

We worship Jesus, because He is the way, the truth and the life.[18] We are to hunger for Him. Paul tells us, "The kingdom of God is not meat and drink; but righteousness, and peace, and joy in the Holy Ghost."[19] The number of times the Bible uses the analogy of food with being hungry for more of God is astounding when we open our eyes and see the truth. Food has become pleasure in our society, but it was meant for fuel.

We are to hunger for Him.

The Message puts it this way. "You're blessed when you've worked up a good appetite for God. He's food and drink in the best meal you'll ever eat."[20] We eat Jesus by taking in His words and they become like food to a dying person. His words fill all of us in a way nothing else can. We drink His living water, truths that give us abundant life and keep us going. No type of physical water even comes close to what His living water can do for us.

Once we get a real taste of what His truth mean to us, we will never want to live any other way. This type of hunger is not physical. It's very, very spiritual.

OPPOSITES DON'T ATTRACT

Personally, I cannot be gorging myself on my favorite foods and be hungry for more of God. There is a great disconnect when I do because I know Jesus has called me to a healthy living journey. I can't be hungry for God and not do what He is directing me to do. I am living a lie when I try to do that. I have to first develop a proper relationship with food before I can really even start to be hungry for Jesus.

Jesus fills us in so many wonderful ways, but we first have to be hungry. I love putting together a lesson for a small group, studying to write a book or preparing to deliver a message. When I have a deadline, it forces me to dig into God's Word, pray, think and meditate. Doing more of that makes me hungry for God's revelation truth. The more I study, the hungrier I become.

In the natural, I live a fasted lifestyle by not eating sugar and gluten. Every time I pass up something made with that combination, I do it as unto God. The more I give these up, the more I don't want them. I can say I am really not hungry for them any more.

I have to reverse that with God's Word. I don't want to go on a fast and not read His Word to feed my soul and spirit. If I do, I will get to the place where I no longer crave Him. I must live from a constant diet of His Word, interaction with Him, messages, podcasts, wonderful Christian music, books, journaling, solitary time with Him, meditation and fellowship with other believers. To not do so would be to die spiritually, just like if I don't eat food, I will die physically.

What I eat physically, though, must be healthy and life-giving. It is the same with what I listen to, read or study. It must be life-giving. I can get a spiritual message out of almost anything if I am full of His Word. His Word must always come first.

I must be hungry for Him not just when I have to speak or write, but every single day, day-in, day-out. His Word must be the lamp[21] that guides me. The only way that can happen is if I am constantly devouring it, ingesting it and letting it feed me spiritually.

APPLICATION

I've learned it's possible to transfer my physical hunger to spiritual hunger when I make being hungry for His Word a priority in my life. I have come to see it for what it is—as necessary to me as eating food that fuels my body and water that makes my body systems operate.

If I am involved in a big project, I can do without a lot of food. Even more amazing is that I cannot do without being immersed in the ways of God either by music, podcast, Scripture, prayer or intentional solitude with Him. It fuels me in an urgent way. Transferring some of my physical hunger to spiritual hunger happens as I integrate Him into my life, talking to Him, listening to His words, singing and praising and writing His truth on my heart.

"So commit yourselves wholeheartedly to these words of Mine. Tie them to your hands and wear them on your forehead as reminders. Teach them to your children. Talk about them when you are at home and when you are on the road, when you are going to bed and when you are getting up. Write them on the doorposts of your house and on your gates, so that as long as the sky remains above the earth, you and your children may flourish in the land the Lord swore to give your ancestors. Be careful to obey all these commands I am giving you. Show love to the LORD your God by walking in His ways and holding tightly to Him."[22]

> To eat His flesh and drink His blood, we must internalize what He tells us and shows us to do.

To eat His flesh and drink His blood, we must internalize what He tells us and shows us to do. We must make it a part of every cell in our bodies. His ways become our ways. He directs everything we do, every step we take.

I thought being hungry would be painful. I didn't want to be empty of food and have a hungry or hollow feeling. However, physically being hungry can be a good thing. It signals our bodies that it is time to eat. If we are never hungry, that means we are always full of food, which is not the best for our physical body. A little hunger is good.

Spiritual hunger is even better, though. It is a driving force that makes us crave knowing God more, to get closer to Him, to fall in love with Him more and more, to obey Him and commit to living His way out of that boundless love He brings to us.

Following Him, then, becomes my life and my source for understanding my destiny. He is more than physical bread and water. He is My Bread of True Life. He is My Living Water. I cannot live without His presence filling all of my life.

Questions

1. How can we crave the sincere milk of the Word? When do you think that would happen or when has it happened in your life? See 1 Peter 2:2 NIV.

_____

_____

_____

2. What would you think if a spiritual teacher began speaking like Jesus was to those gathered and telling them what He did in John 6:48-49? Put yourself in their places. Would you stay or leave? Why or why not?

_____

_____

_____

3. Why did Jesus produce a miracle and feed the 5,000? What point was He trying to make?

_____

_____

_____

4. Why was Jesus a little upset with those who followed Him across the sea? What did He say it showed they wanted? Do we do the same thing when we follow churches or pastors who promise us stuff? What kinds of things have you followed or seen others follow a movement for?

_____

_____

_____

5. What does Jesus say should be the reason they should follow Him?

_____

_____

_____

6. What does hungering and thirsting for Jesus mean to you?

_____

_____

_____

7. What does Jesus mean when He says we are to take up our cross daily? What would taking up your cross look like in your everyday life? What would you be doing? What would you not be doing?

_____

_____

_____

8. How can you become so hungry for God that you crave Him more than you crave your trigger foods, those that set you off on a binge?

_____

_____

_____

9. Read Psalm 63:5 NLT: "You satisfy me more than the richest feast. I will praise You with songs of joy." How can God satisfy you like a rich feast?

_____

_____

_____

Activity

SCRIPTURE: "So commit yourselves wholeheartedly to these words of Mine. Tie them to your hands and wear them on your forehead as reminders. Teach them to your children. Talk about them when you are at home and when you are on the road, when you are going to bed and when you are getting up. Write them on the doorposts of your house and on your gates, so that as long as the sky remains above the earth, you and your children may flourish in the land the LORD swore to give your ancestors. Be careful to obey all these commands I am giving you. Show love to the LORD your God by walking in His ways and holding tightly to Him." —Deut. 11:28-30 NLT.

SUPPLIES: Glue, double-stick tape, old magazines, catalogs or newspapers, scraps of material, things from nature, old jewelry, buttons, dried flowers, etc. Poster board if not utilizing the empty page in the book.

CREATE A COLLAGE: Using the blank page in this book, make a collage centered around a meaningful Scripture verse, perhaps from this chapter. Instead of creating the collage in your book, you may wish to use a sturdy poster board in the size that works for you. And use the page here for planning your collage.

For your collage you will need some super glue, wood glue or craft glue to attach items to the page or your poster board. Double-stick tape also works well.

Gather items to use. Cut pictures or words cut out of magazines, catalogs or newspapers. Find scraps of material or old articles of clothing you can cut pieces from. Many items work for collages. It all depends on the idea you want to create. Items might include buttons, pieces of wood, metal, old jewelry, aluminum foil, leaves, acorns, branches, feathers, dried flowers. With this project, the sky is the limit.

To begin, cover the background of your poster with paint or watercolor or leave it white if you prefer. Choose your Scripture. Print this out in a decorative font of some kind using a good printer or hand letter it on a piece of colored paper or paper of your choosing. Put this either in the center, at the top or bottom of your collage as the anchor.

Now glue on the other items you have found. Add things that speak to you and in some way illustrate your scripture. Specific photos or words from magazine can add to this, but also various other things you find. This can be a great reminder of the One you serve.

More Inspiration

Make a bead bracelet choosing colors to remind you of God's attributes. Help your child or another child memorize a Scripture. Begin a prayer walk with a friend praying over a certain neighborhood as you walk. Make a poster or graphic on your computer. Frame it and hang where everyone who comes into your home can see it.

My Collage

CHAPTER 5—BEING FED BY THE MASTER

ENDNOTES

1. 1 Peter 2:2 NIV
2. John 6:48-51 NLT
3. John 6:53-58 NLT
4. John 6:61-63 NASB
5. John 6:68-69 NASB
6. John 6:2 NASB
7. John 6:5 NASB
8. John 6:9 NASB
9. Mark 6:37 NASB
10. Mark 6:40-44 NASB
11. John 6:14 NIV
12. John 6:25 NASB
13. John 6:26-27 NASB
14. John 6:35 NASB
15. John 6:40 NASB
16. Luke 9:23 NLT
17. 1 Cor. 6:13 NASB
18. John 14:6 NIV
19. Romans 14:17 KJV
20. Matthew 5:6 MSG
21. Psalm 119:105 NIV
22. Duet. 11:18-22 NLT

The Battle Is The Lord's

There is a mountain in front of me.
A giant problem I cannot face
and cannot overcome.
I wish I had the faith of David
that one short climb or small stone
could solve everything.
But I can't climb and I don't have a slingshot.
My skills seem few
And my desire wanes.

God, where do I go to buy faith?
Can you impart it to me
or does it only come with hard work?
I feel I don't have time to figure it out.
I want the mountain, the giant,
to be gone from my life.
But not even climbing shoes and slingshots
can take care of the issues
that have plagued me forever.

I do understand, God, that You have the power
to move mountains, slay giants
and do the impossible.
Would you do that for me now, God?
Would you come and in Your presence
would You still my anxious heart?
Would You calm my fears?
I believe You when You say
You are the God of the impossible.

This battle I'm fighting,
this relentless battle,
I'm giving up and handing it to You.
I've tried everything and I'm done.
I will do it Your way.
You are the way, the truth and the life.
I am slowly dying. I need life today.
Come, God, fight this battle for me.
The victory will not be mine, but Yours.

CHAPTER 6

LUNCH FOR THE SOLDIERS

———⁓———————————⁓———

Provision is one of our basic needs as human beings. We come into this world as helpless infants. Even Jesus had to be raised by earthly parents. Hand-picked by God, Mary and Joseph took care of Jesus. He nursed at Mary's breast. He ate the food provided by his step-father Joseph. He grew in wisdom and in stature.[1] That means both His mind and body grew from the teaching and caretaking of his parents.

If we don't have our basic needs met early in life it short-circuits something in us. We've had 10 foster children and young adults live in our home through the years. Without fail, they fall into two categories—as babies and children they either didn't know where their next meal was coming from or they had parents who did provide for them in that area, but couldn't continue because of illness, poor health or other issues.

Those who had parents who couldn't provide for them early in life were difficult to reassure that they didn't have to hoard food or belongings. Those who had parents or others who provided had an easier time of adapting to our home. It didn't matter that we had plenty of food on the table at every meal, in the refrigerator and in the cabinets, those who had an early disconnect with provision would still try to sneak food and hide it in their rooms or worse yet, cram entire packages of bologna down their throats to a disastrous result shortly afterwards.

It's hard to reassure someone there will be food when all they've known as infants and children is lack. It gets ingrained in them early. It's in their neural pathways and they have no idea of how to combat the urge to hide and hoard food.

Good parents provide for their children and take care of them.

Good parents provide for their children and take care of them. Therefore, it is natural that Jesse sent his youngest son, David, to take food to his older brothers who were fighting the Philistines. It is so natural that we tend to skip over this fact when we read the well-known story of David and Goliath.

"One day Jesse said to David, 'Take this basket of roasted grain and these 10 loaves of bread, and carry them quickly to your brothers. And give these 10 cuts of cheese to their captain. See how your brothers are getting along, and bring back a report on how they are doing.'"[2]

By this time, Jesse was old, and David was home taking care of the family sheep business. His older brothers were fighting in the Israeli army, but David, a strong teenager, was doing his duty to his father. He understood his place was at home.

David's father knew there was something special David would one day be called to do. As a small boy he had been anointed by Samuel to be the king of Israel.

Did David understand the ramifications of this? It's not clear from scripture if he did or didn't. Jesse knew, though. How could a father not remember the prophet Samuel coming to his home and going one by one down the line of his sons. Surely Jesse remembered Samuel's words to him. "The Lord has not chosen any of these."[3]

He also remembered when Samuel asked for Jesse's youngest son, the dutiful one taking care of the sheep and goats in the field, to be sent for. "Send for him at once," Samuel said. "We will not sit down to eat until he arrives."[4] In other words it was of utmost importance that Samuel meet David.

THE ANOINTING

"So Jesse sent for him. He was dark and handsome, with beautiful eyes. And the Lord said, 'This is the one. Anoint him.' So as David stood there among his brothers, Samuel took the flask of olive oil he had brought and anointed David with the oil. And the Spirit of the Lord came powerfully upon David from that day on."[5]

Jesse knew his youngest son was special, however he did not treat him any different. His father seemed determined to simply hold the memories in his heart and train his son to be faithful to the tasks at hand.

The anointing ceremony probably did play a part in Jesse later allowing David to stay in the service of King Saul. God's Spirit left Saul and the Lord sent a tormenting spirit that filled

Saul with depression and fear. Saul's servants sent for David who was known as one who could play the harp well to come and play soothing music to help Saul.

It worked so well that Saul asked Jesse if David could remain in his service because "whenever the tormenting spirit from God troubled Saul, David would play the harp. Then Saul would feel better, and the tormenting spirit would go away."[6] Jesse allowed his youngest son to stay as long as Saul needed him.

Some time must have passed between 1 Samuel 16 and 17 because David was no longer a boy. As the youngest of Jesse's sons, though, he was back home in Bethlehem helping his aged father manage the family business. He did whatever his father told him to do and that led him to take lunch to his older brothers and check on their welfare. His brothers were men fighting in a war. It probably wasn't just a lunch pail. It was a pack of provision.

David was attentive to the details of the assignment.

David was attentive to all the details of the assignment. Before he left to take the provisions to his brothers, he found someone to watch the sheep.[7] Once he arrived at camp, he saw the Israeli army lining up for battle against the Philistines. He knew his brothers were probably there, so he left what he brought with the keeper of supplies and hurried out to find them.[8]

David could have been haughty about his place. He could have made demands on those around him. After all he was going to be king some day. Many fathers would have made sure their son knew that, but that's not how his father raised him. He raised him to manage himself well and take care of the tasks he'd been assigned. He raised him to live a normal life.

What David saw and heard disturbed him. He saw a Philistine giant. Estimates are that he stood over 11 feet tall and that his armor alone weighed over 125 pounds. The monster was taunting the Israelites to send even one man to fight him.

His daily challenge was, "Choose one man to come down here and fight me! If he kills me, then we will be your slaves. But if I kill him, you will be our slaves! I defy the armies of Israel today! Send me a man who will fight me!"[9] Saul was by far the tallest and most skilled of the Israelites, but even he was "terrified and deeply shaken"[10] by Goliath's words.

ENTER THE ANOINTED

A righteous anger was stirred inside David. He began inquiring about what he would receive if he were to fight Goliath and win. He was told that the king had offered a huge reward to anyone who killed him. He would receive one of the king's daughters as a wife and the man's entire family would be exempted from paying taxes. News of David's inquiries got back to the king and Saul sent for him.

When David went to see Saul it was not clear if Saul remembered David as the psalmist who served in his court as a smaller boy. He called him "only a boy" when he saw him, but some time had passed and David had grown up. He revealed character, strength of Spirit and experience to Saul in several things he unabashedly said to the King of Israel.

"Don't worry about this Philistine. I'll go fight him ... I have been taking care of my father's sheep and goats. When a lion or a bear comes to steal a lamb from the flock, I go after it with a club and rescue the lamb from its mouth. If the animal turns on me, I catch it by the jaw and club it to death. I have done this to both lions and bears and I'll do it to this pagan Philistine, too, for he has defied the armies of the living God. The Lord who rescued me from the claws of the lion and the bear will rescue me from this Philistine."[11]

> David brought his brothers lunch, but with lunch he also brought the presence of God.

David brought his brothers lunch, but with lunch he also brought the presence of God. That day all he had to do was face the giant knowing from experience God would do the impossible. God would deliver the monster of a man into David's hands. Of that David was more than sure.

David figured Goliath couldn't be any more imposing than a bear or lion. Bears in that area might be 550 pounds and over six feet tall.[12] Lions were known for their ferocity and driven nature. They were also large, though, with the largest African lion ever recorded being 11 feet long and 800 pounds and the largest Asian lion being around 9.5 feet long and over 400 pounds.[13]

Saul was impressed with what David had accomplished. Saul had never killed a lion or a bear and certainly not in hand-to-hand combat or with just a club. Not only that, David had a determination about him that said he was not afraid.

David knew it would not be in his strength that he would kill Goliath, but in God's strength.

What's even more remarkable, though, was that Saul put Israel's entire fate in the hands of this bold, teenage shepherd. He was desperate. If David won the battle, the Philistines would be Israel's slaves, but if Goliath won all of Israel would be their slaves. It looked like Israel would lose either way, but not without a fight no matter how unfair the battle looked. Faced with sending someone into battle, he decided to send the only one willing to die and that was the shepherd-boy, harp-player, a very unlikely hero of war.

David was the only one who hadn't been programmed for 40 days with the fear of the size and the roar of the Philistine giant. The words hadn't been embedded in his brain and hadn't had time to produce fear, just indignation that this man would dare set himself up above what David knew to be the will of God. The Israelites were not just afraid of Goliath, they were literally cowering behind their shields. He was huge and they felt tiny and insignificant in comparison.

David, however, was not afraid and did not cower behind a shield or bulky armor that would slow him down. He faced Goliath as himself with the weapons he had used before and was well acquainted with—five smooth stones from the creek. Goliath was tall and his head was large. David chose stones proportioned to fit right between the giant's eyes. They had to be exactly the right size. How did he know that? He knew it from experience. When bringing down a lion or a bear, he knew he only had one shot.

He also knew the element of surprise had to be in his favor with Goliath.

DAVID'S DECLARATION

David told Goliath in no uncertain terms that God was going to bring him down that day. He said, "Today the Lord will conquer you, and I will kill you and cut off your head. And then I will give the dead bodies of your men to the birds and wild animals, and the whole world will know that there is a God in Israel! And everyone assembled here will know that the Lord rescues His people, but not with sword and spear. This is the Lord's battle, and He will give you to us!"[14]

That day God triumphed over the largest man Israel had ever seen with perhaps one of the smallest men there. If there is a significance to the fact that David picked up five stones, it was that the supernatural would always win over the natural, as the number five is the number of natural man.

As Goliath lumbered closer to try to attack David, the younger, more limber and spry man ran with the wind of the Spirit and took Goliath off guard by hurling the perfect stone from his slingshot. It was a dead-on hit to the giant's forehead and he face-planted into the ground.

That wasn't enough for David. He made good on his promise. Taking Goliath's sword, he cut off the giant's head. When the Philistines saw their champion was dead, they turned and ran. The Israeli army chased them and defeated them that day.

David had told Goliath the truth, it was the Lord's battle. He conquered Goliath for Israel.

After the victory of the Israeli army, David once again played the harp for Saul. Only now Saul was jealous of David. He had made him a commander of the army and the people loved him. They sang, "Saul has killed his thousands and David his ten thousands."[15] Saul was spitting mad.

As David was playing the harp, Saul threw a spear at him. David avoided it twice. Finally Saul was just plain afraid of David and tried to send him into battle to die. This plan failed as all of Saul's plans eventually did. They failed because as Saul himself knew, the Lord's presence and anointing was with David wherever he went and whatever he did.

A big part of this was because David was and would always be, no matter what sin he committed, "a man after God's own heart."[16]

APPLICATION

In David's diligence of bringing physical provision for his soldier brothers, he brought so much more. He brought the very presence of God. This was no surprise to the shepherd. He had no doubt God was with him.

It was a concept that Saul and his army did not believe. As a matter of fact, Saul knew God had left him. He especially knew it after the shepherd boy killed the Philistine giant when he, the king, was too afraid to even try.

David was simply doing the work his father had asked him to do. In being willing to do that one task, a nation was saved. In addition, David was elevated to the notoriety that would eventually crown him king of Israel, a king who would restore Israel to a land ruled by the hand of God.

That day David was focused on the task at hand, taking lunch to his brothers—food, provision and their welfare. All physical needs went by the wayside when he saw the dire threat not only they were under, but all of Israel as well. They had deeper needs than what was for lunch. Their very lives were on the line.

He could have simply taken lunch and returned to his father. Instead he took the anointing he knew God had given him and stood up to one of the greatest dangers Israel had ever faced. This became personal. It was an individual threat to each man in the Israeli army. For 40 days Goliath had been challenging not just Israel, but each man in the army. "Are you man enough to fight me?" Every day each man had to face the fact that they felt emasculated by the sheer thought of facing such a giant.

> God's supernatural power was with them just like He promised.

The fact is no one, not even David, was capable of winning over Goliath. The giant was the largest of men. He had the most armor. He was destined to win. It was a done deal. In everyone's mind, the battle was already over.

They had not factored in that God was still with those who believed. His supernatural power was with them just like He promised. It took one who not only knew the truth, but had experienced that truth first-hand to defeat the giant.

In another instance Jesus said something similar to His followers. "If you stick with this, living out what I tell you, you are my disciples for sure. Then you will experience for yourselves the truth, and the truth will free you."[17]

No one can take our experiences from us. David had to rely on God when alone with the sheep. He took his job seriously. He protected the sheep with his very life with blind faith in God coming to his rescue in the face of overwhelming odds. Seriously, a bear and a lion up against a boy? Who would win? Ah, but God … we always seem to leave Him out of the equation.

The battle is not ours. It is the Lord's.

The lunch David brought was forgotten. God's presence and victory was all that mattered that day. Every day we need fuel. We need food. We need provision, but more significantly we need God every moment of every hour.

He is provision for what is facing us even if it is just an ordinary day of making lunch for the family. What might that lead to? We never know, but we must always and forever, be aware that there is a deeper truth at work here.

David carried God's presence with him. We have that same Spirit, the Spirit of God, living in us always if we have accepted Jesus as our Savior. We have the scale-tipper, chain-breaker, way-maker living inside of us.

It's the same Spirit David called on to walk by faith and not by sight[18] that day He faced Goliath. It's the same Spirit who raised Christ from the dead.[19]

My giant was my extreme weight issue. Others may have another issue that looms like a giant in their lives, a mountain that seems impossible to move. Whatever we are facing we need only understand and fully comprehend, the battle is not ours. It is the Lord's.[20]

Questions

1. As a mother I'm always concerned that my family has enough to eat and I know my husband is concerned that we have enough money to buy food. Are there some things more important than food? List them.

   _____

   _____

   _____

2. How can we begin to change our mindset? What would that look like for you and your family?

   _____

   _____

   _____

3. What do you think Jesse was trying to teach David? How did he do that?

   _____

   _____

   _____

4. Why do you think David stood up to the bear and lion in the first place?

_____

_____

_____

5. Why did David, a mere teenager, get involved in a war of epic proportions? What was he thinking?

_____

_____

_____

6. Why did Goliath make him so mad? List every way you can think of.

_____

_____

_____

7. What weapons do we try to use to fight our battles? Can you apply any of the lessons you learned from David to winning the battles in your own life? How did David defeat the giant?

_____

_____

_____

8. What characterizes a person after God's heart? List some characteristics that come to you.

_____

_____

_____

9. How can ordinary tasks like making lunch for your family become extraordinary?

_____

_____

_____

10. What giant or giants are you facing in your life? What looms as overwhelming and impossible to you right now? How can you view your situation with spiritual eyes and walk by faith not by how the situation appears?

_____

_____

_____

SCRIPTURE: "Jesus looked at them and said, 'With man this is impossible, but with God all things are possible.'" —Matthew 19:26 NIV

SUPPLIES: Pen.

DEFEATING THE GIANTS: On the page provided draw an outline of the giant you are facing in your life right now. It can be anything. In my life I've had many, but two that come to mind are weighing 430 pounds and having a huge debt including cars, home mortgage and credit card bills.

Both of these seemed to be something that could never be eradicated. They seemed to be set in stone and immovable. Yours may be entirely different. It can be an addiction, a relationship issue, a job issue, lack of education or any number of things.

Draw an outline to symbolize this giant. For example, I would draw an outline of a large blob of a woman. Some might draw a large cigarette, large bottle of alcohol, a large pile of money, the outline of a house or car or group of people. You get the idea. Remember, just an outline because you need to leave space around the outside of your giant and inside the giant to write.

Around the outside of the outline list all the things that contributed to this giant materializing in your life. In the case of my weight issue, most of it would be various foods, but there would also be core issues of being molested and feeling the need to be protected, feeling the need to comfort and reward myself, wanting to be loved and feeling emotionally empty, wanting to be understood and have companions who understood me, etc. All of those would be outside issues that contributed to the growth of my giant.

The most important step is next. Inside the giant, draw a rectangular box. Inside the box you are going to make a list. Number it 1-5 and leave space for making a list.

Before the list, though, around the outside of the box and inside the giant, write the scriptures and insights, which will help you conquer or overcome this giant. Possible Scriptures to include might be: Matthew 19:26, Matthew 17:20 or Philippians 4:13. Include those meaningful to you.

Include things you know to be true, such as Jesus is Lord or the Holy Spirit is my power source. Write things that help you know this giant can be brought down.

Pray and ask God to give you five action steps to bring down the giant with God's help. These steps will go inside the box. You now have an action plan to begin to defeat your giant. You may just want brief words to remind you of the action step. I would write stop, listen, pray, follow, praise.

Now, you have reasons why the giant became a giant in the first place. Some of these you may need to repent of. Some you may need to forgive others for by just stating out loud to God, "I forgive this person for this issue."

You also have scriptural promises to stand firm on. What more do you need but a slingshot to bring that sucker down?

Defeating My Giants

More Inspiration

Find five smooth stones. You can collect them from your yard or get them at a discount or hobby store. If you buy them they come in bags of various sizes. On the bottom of each stone in permanent marker write one word that describes the giant that is looming in your life. I would have written "430 Pounds."

As you write your word on the bottom of the stone pray and say, "I hand this giant of _____ in my life to You. What do You give me in exchange"

Set the stone down on a table and write the thing He gives you on top of the stone. This will be something to help you defeat your giant.

Now, turn the stone over and with your permanent marker blot out the word signifying your giant. Alternatively, you can get some felt. Cut it in the shape of the bottom of the stone. Glue the felt over the word signifying your giant. Magically, the giant is gone and in its place is the word God gave you to help the giant stay gone!

ENDNOTES

1. Luke 2:52 NIV
2. 1 Samuel 17:17-18 NLT
3. 1 Samuel 16:10 NLT
4. 1 Samuel 16:11 NLT
5. 1 Samuel 16:12-13 NLT
6. 1 Samuel 16:23 NLT
7. 1 Samuel 17:20 NLT
8. 1 Samuel 17:22 NLT
9. 1 Samuel 17:8-10 NLT
10. 1 Samuel 17:11 NLT
11. 1 Samuel 17:32, 34-37 NLT
12. "Syrian Brown Bear – Ursus Arctos Syriacus – Bears Of The World." *Syrian Brown Bear – Ursus Arctos Syriacus –Bears Of The World.* N.p., n.d. Web 18 Jan. 2017.
13. "How Big Is the Largest Lion Ever Recorded?" *Reference.* N.p., n.d. Web. 18 Jan. 2017.
14. 1 Samuel 17:46-47 NLT
15. 1 Samuel 18:7 NLT
16. Acts 13:22 NLT
17. John 8:32 MSG
18. 2 Cor. 5:7 NKJV
19. Romans 8:11 NIV
20. 1 Samuel 17:47 NLT

The Wedding

White and red roses in place.
Purity, redemption the theme.
Violins softly played Amazing Grace.
The guests were seated in wait.

All eyes on the Groom dressed in white.
His shoulders bore the crimson robe.
On His head jewels and a crown of light.
All was ready for His glorious Bride.

As the orchestra played on
guests whispered their dismay
wondering if the bride had gone
as flowers wilted in the sun.

On this very special day
the orchestra was getting tired.
What could be the delay
the guests wondered with a yawn?

One by one they began to leave
with the orchestra close behind.
Would the couple not to each other cleave?
Caterers were shooed away.

Yet the Bridegroom stood strong
waiting for His Bride to come.
Knowing she to Him did belong.
And He is waiting for me still.

CHAPTER 7

WHAT'S FOR
SUPPER?

While I was growing up we were in church every time the doors were open. Sunday morning, and Sunday, Wednesday and Friday nights were the regular meeting times. My dad was always there on the second row to the right. That meant I was there as well. Church was definitely like another home to me. I loved going, especially during revival time.

One reason I looked forward to the special services was because of the great dishes that would always be available at the carry-in dinners afterwards. There was plenty of food like hot homemade bread and rolls, roast and gravy, dumplings, real mashed potatoes, special cakes, brownies, cookies and fruit salad with cream cheese, nuts and marshmallows.

I liked my church family, but truth be told, it was the meal during revival or any Sunday dinner that I loved. During revival week we had those dinners after every meeting. The evangelist had to eat and we could all join in.

The guest preacher would invariably pound out a fire and brimstone message about the Marriage Supper of the Lamb.[1] I could easily understand a supper or feast, as they sometimes called it.

I could just imagine everyone getting together in Heaven at this really long, beautiful table. They could eat anything and everything they wanted.[2] Because I loved to eat, I really would be in Heaven.

It would be a non-stop reunion with all the foods I knew and loved.

The reason for having such a message during a revival was to let those who hadn't accepted Christ[3] know they wouldn't get to come to this supper. It was to get them to think about what they would be missing.

All of this escaped my attention because in my mind, I was back at the feast chowing down. For sure I wanted to be there. What better way to reward those who said the prayer and accepted Jesus than by a huge feast with all our favorite foods? Even better, we'd get to eat for a long time.

I heard something about seven years and that seemed like forever. It would be in Heaven so that was definitely possible. Certainly, I wanted to be there. It would be a non-stop reunion with all the foods I knew and loved.

As a child I didn't stop and wonder about this. I just knew what a supper was and since it would be in Heaven, it just made sense to me that it would an unending time of delicious delicacies. I couldn't wait!

WHO'S GETTING MARRIED?

This marriage supper is a celebration of a wedding so who is the bride? Who is the bridegroom? And who are the guests? Of course, Jesus is the bridegroom.

In Matthew 24, Jesus was instructing His disciples about the signs of the end times, the Great Tribulation and the Second Coming. He told them no one knows when the Son of Man will come again.

In a short parable of the faithful servant and the evil servant, He admonished them to be watchful and make sure they stayed true to what they knew they should be doing.

In Matthew 25, Jesus continued with the parable of the 10 virgins, five of them were wise (far-sighted, practical and sensible) and five were foolish (thoughtless, silly and careless).[4] During the Jewish wedding ceremonies of that time, the bride did not know when the bridegroom would come for her. Therefore, when he came, the wedding began. She had to be ready and watching.

In this parable there were five virgins who were prepared and ready for their weddings. They had oil with them.[5] The five who were foolish took no oil with them.[6] Really, who does that? Who goes to get married and isn't prepared for the fact the bridegroom might be delayed, especially because in the Jewish culture that happened all the time?

> She had to be ready and watching.

When the cry sounded that the bridegroom was coming, the foolish panicked and had to go buy oil. "And while they went to buy, the bridegroom came, and those who were ready went in with him to the wedding; and the door was shut ... Watch therefore, for you know neither the day nor the hour in which the Son of Man is coming."[7]

It's clear from this passage that the bride, who has been referred to as the church in many passages,[8] is those in the church who are prepared and ready to be united to the bridegroom. This would be those who are eagerly anticipating His arrival because they have been preparing.

PREPARATIONS

What would those preparations look like? How would we, as members of the body of Christ, prepare to unite with Him and become His bride for all of eternity? One thing I know is if I was getting married, I would want to get to know my bridegroom as well as possible. I'd want to know His ways, His preferences and the kinds of things He would expect from His bride. I'd want to know these things because I loved Him.

I would want to be spending time with Him now instead of waiting for something to magically happen for all of eternity just because I said a prayer when I was seven. I'd want to understand what is required from me in the role of His helpmate for all of eternity.

Even though I need to be ready for my bridegroom, He has already been preparing me, as a part of the church, to be His bride. His love has made me holy through the washing of the water through the Word, and He is presenting me to Himself as a part of the radiant church, without stain or wrinkle or any other blemish, but holy and blameless.[9]

That doesn't mean I shouldn't be prepared, it just means I need to accept His supreme sacrifice for me and return to Him my love and adoration.

WILL THERE BE FOOD IN HEAVEN?

The truth hit me quite suddenly one day. I probably won't be hungry in Heaven. I'm not even sure there will be or need to be food there. I don't know for sure what our resurrected bodies will need, but I just can't see food, money, sleep, clothes or any of the things we value so highly here on earth being important while we live in Jesus' presence. We won't even notice the absence of our favorite foods.

So why in the world does the book of Revelation talk about this huge feast? As I went back to look at the passage I saw that these verses are really not about eating. These verses are about celebrating for a period of time until the marriage is complete. Until we, as the church, are joined with the bridegroom. It says nothing about food. There's only one mention of anything edible—the Lamb.

> We won't even notice the absence of our favorite foods.

"Then I heard again what sounded like the shout of a vast crowd or the roar of mighty ocean waves or the crash of loud thunder: 'Praise the Lord. For the Lord our God, the Almighty, reigns. Let us be glad and rejoice, and let us give honor to Him. For the time has come for the wedding feast of the Lamb, and His bride has prepared herself. She has been given the finest of pure white linen to wear. For the fine linen represents the good deeds of God's holy people.'

"And the angel said to me, 'Write this: Blessed are those who are invited to the wedding feast of the Lamb.' And he added, 'These are true words that come from God.'"[10]

> The marriage supper is the illustration of our final union with Christ, the Redeemer.

The Jewish people were just like us in that when they wanted to celebrate, they fed everyone in a big way. They partied and ate for a week after any wedding ceremony took place.

They got out their finest plates and linens, served the best wine and killed the choicest livestock. A wedding was something the entire community celebrated and took time away from their regular work to enjoy.

There was dancing, music and laughter. It was what they did for fun. It was an event to which they looked forward.

God used this illustration of the wedding to drive home a point. The bridegroom is the perfect, spotless lamb, who was slain so that those who believe in Him do not have to live forever in torment. The bride is the church, those of us who are sinners and have accepted Christ's sacrifice for our sins.

The marriage supper is the illustration of our final union with Christ, the Redeemer. He will appear as the Lamb who was slain because it's in that role that we understand His supreme love for us.[11] It is the time when He not only presents, but accepts us as His forever bride. It will be a day of rejoicing the likes of which we have never seen before.

APPLICATION

The Marriage Supper of the Lamb is not about what we are going to be eating. It's not about eating as much of Aunt Cora Lee's pies and cakes as we want and never gaining an ounce or going back for seconds and thirds of Aunt Betty's dumplings and never feeling gorged. It's not about eating chicken fried steak, mashed potatoes and gravy for seven years straight and not having to let our robes out.

While we are here on earth we see things in earthly terms that we can understand. We think about how a feast will satisfy our physical and emotional needs. The idea of the marriage supper, in my mind, is simply a way to tell us there will be a celebration in Heaven when we get there and are continually in the presence of our Savior. It has nothing to do with filling our needs or desires. Even though the marriage supper is a celebration and in earthly terms, food is not a part of it.

In the ultimate wedding supper, though, one of the reasons Jesus appears in His role as the Lamb is because He is our food and our portion. Much like we need food to live and eat it in the right portions, we need Jesus to live. As scripture says, "'The LORD is my portion and my inheritance,' says my soul; 'Therefore I have hope in Him *and* wait expectantly for Him.'"[12] The portion of Jesus we get

> The portion we get of Jesus is unlimited.

is unlimited. We celebrate Him continually. We covenant with Him for eternity. We abide in His presence always.

Grandma's oatmeal cookies will be the last thing on our minds. Thinking of ways we can show honor and praise to the One who deserves it all will consume us. Time will fade. We will be caught up in His glory, grace and majesty. We will be basking in an unending time of His presence.

It reminds me of a commercial I saw recently. It shows a wedding and all the festivities including the wedding reception and dinner. The bride and groom are greeting everyone and having lots of fun, but they never have a chance to eat their meal. As a matter of fact, that doesn't even seem to be on their minds.

They get in the limo to be whisked away on their honeymoon. As they sit down, they find a meal waiting for them with a note from the bride's dad. "Eating's the last thing on your mind when it's your wedding."

It's a feast, but it's not about the food. It's about union with our Savior.

It's a truth I could not have grasped even a few years ago. Nothing was more important to me than the things I ate and craved.

Nothing was more important than the next big event when I could eat as much of my favorites as I wanted. I gauged whether I would attend an event by what kind of food would be served and who was making it.

Now I realize, nothing is more important to me than hearing the voice of my Savior, being in His presence, knowing He knows me and following what He tells me.[13]

I desire that union, that marriage with Him, to know His mind completely, to understand the mysteries of the universe, to follow Him for eternity.

To be close to Him forever will be my food and portion. "His compassions fail not. They are new every morning. Great is your faithfulness. 'The Lord is my portion,' says my soul. 'Therefore I will hope in Him.'"[14]

> He is my everything, my all in all, my portion.

He is my everything.[15] He is my all in all.[16] He is my portion.[17] He is more than enough.[18] No large piece of the best red velvet cake will ever compete.

As a matter of fact, nothing else will come close to being in His Presence, united with Him forever.

And no one will say, "What's for supper?"

Questions

1. What do you think of when you hear the Marriage Supper of the Lamb?

   _____

   _____

   _____

2. What are the qualifications to be the bride? See Matthew 25:1-10.

   _____

   _____

   _____

3. What does Ephesians 5:25-28 NIV mean to you? What does thinking of yourself as the bride in this passage mean to you?

   _____

   _____

   _____

4. Do you think there will be food in Heaven? How about money? Sleep? Clothes? Sex? Defend your answer.

_____

_____

_____

5. Read Revelation 19:6-9 out loud. What stands out to you?

_____

_____

_____

6. Why will Jesus appear as the Lamb? What does that mean to you? See 1 John 3:16.

_____

_____

_____

7. What does it mean to you that you will be the bride of Christ? Is this a role you look forward to?

_____

_____

_____

8. Looking forward to this day is wonderful, but who is Jesus to us today? How can we get to know Him better today?

_____

_____

_____

9. In what ways can we seek to be totally united with our Savior while here on earth?

_____

_____

_____

10. What might keep you from arriving at the wedding? In what way is Jesus waiting on you?

_____

_____

_____

11. How can Jesus become your food and your portion? See Lamentations 3:22-24 AMP.

_____

_____

_____

12. Play the song, "I Can Only Imagine" by Mercy Me. What will you do first when you get to Heaven? What is the first thing you want to ask Him?

_____

_____

_____

Activity

SCRIPTURE: "Then I heard again what sounded like the shout of a vast crowd or the roar of mighty ocean waves or the crash of loud thunder: 'Praise the Lord! For the Lord, the Almighty, reigns. Let us be glad and rejoice, and let us give honor to Him. For the time has come for the wedding feast of the Lamb, and His bride has prepared herself. She has been given the finest of pure white linen to wear.' For linen represents the good deeds of God's holy people." —Revelation 19: 6-8 NLT

SUPPLIES: Pen

WRITE A POEM: Put on some quiet worship music. Spend time soaking in God's presence. When you are ready, write a love poem to Jesus. Make it personal. Address what it means to have intimacy with Jesus, to be married to Him. When Jesus says He is the bridegroom and we are the bride what does that mean to you?

A poem can be a prose poem, which is words that illustrate feelings. It can be rhyming, but does not have to be. Don't worry about theology. Write from your heart. It could be a love sonnet to your bridegroom, who is Jesus. It could be telling Him what things you are giving up to be totally united with Him. Just express your love and praises to Jesus.

The Bridegroom

Write a poem or write down words about what it would be like to have Jesus as your Bridegroom. What does that mean to you? What kind of wedding would it be?

_____

_____

_____

_____

_____

_____

_____

_____

_____

_____

_____

_____

_____

More Inspiration

Jesus uses the illustration of a wedding to symbolize our union with Him. Think about the various symbols in a wedding, yours, someone else's or those you've seen or heard about, including the wedding dress, colors, the rings, vows, songs other elements of the service, the wedding reception and any other events. Whether it was a perfect wedding or not, what should a wedding symbolize?

Attach copies of photos or photos from magazines to a poster or page in your journal. Use pictures from your wedding or someone else's to help you remember picture what being married to Jesus might mean.

Write notes to yourself about what you thought about as you did this exercise.

ENDNOTES

1. Revelation 19:7 NLT

2. Note: There are various interpretations of when and where the Marriage Supper of the Lamb will take place. For purposes of this chapter I share my childhood recollections of what I heard pastors say. I'd like to believe the church will be raptured before the tribulation and we will be in Heaven celebrating, but I'm well aware that could be entirely wrong. It is my firm belief, though, that such an event will take place sometime, somewhere. Heaven sounds like a great place for that to occur, however I refuse to get into an end times discussion. I can argue both sides, but what's the point? My salvation does not depend on knowing that. As a matter of fact Scripture says in Matthew 24:36 that we won't know when Jesus will return. What happens will happen in God's time. He's the only one who knows and that's good enough for me.

3. John 3:16 NLT

4. Matthew 25:2 AMP

5. Matthew 25:4 NKJV

6. Matthew 25:3 NKJV

7. Matthew 25:10, 13 NKJV

8. 2 Corinthians 11:2 NIV, Isaiah 54:5-6 NIV

9. Ephesians 5:26-28 NIV

10. Revelation 19:6-9 NLT

11. 1 John 3:16 NIV

12. Lamentations 3:24 AMP

13. John 10:27 NIV

14. Lamentations 3:24 NKJV

15. Colossians 1:18 NIV

16. Colossians 1:17 NIV

17. Psalm 73:26 NKJV

18. 2 Cor. 12:9 MSG

Surrendered to His Design

I am trapped in a cavernous, never-ending place.
My exercise is finding whatever encloses me.
It is dark and scary here as I feel my way along the wall.
I am angry. I scream in pain, anguish that no one hears.
I cry tears of regret—deep, gut-wrenching tears.

I am paying penance for being me.
I accept responsibility. It weighs on my mind.
It overwhelms me and yet, I cannot lay it down.
It defines me and has become my existence.
I just exist. I do not live.

But I can no longer stand under the weight of me.
I listen and recognize the Voice I know well.
He speaks through those I know offering hands of freedom.
Within me begins to well up new feelings of hope.
I see a trickle of light in the darkness.

As the Light floods this place I start to recognize
Deep gashes, slashes of open, oozing wounds I know well.
As my eyes focus on each, the Voice says, "Hand them to Me."
I watch amazed as the hurts and pains of the past heal.
In their place, gold starts to form.

Each wound unveils more hidden treasure.
There is gold inside me. This one says strong.
Another courageous, peaceful, patient, full of grace and faith.
I am a woman with gifts. They start to surface and yet,
I cannot use these in my solitude.

I search for the way out, a door, an opening to freedom.
More light is available now and I ask for the way.
How do I step away from this place I have created?
Over there—a strong shaft of Light.
It is a shape I know well. It is the shape of ... my heart.

I am defined by Light. He has made beauty from my ashes.
I comforted myself with my self-imposed addictions.
I gave myself what I wanted, but it was not what I needed.
All along I needed His revelation design for me.
The Light has made me whole.

I live to do God's bidding here on this earth.
I live to worship and praise the God who healed me.
I live to bring freedom to others.
I live to be a trophy of God's grace.
I live surrendered to His design.

CHAPTER 8

HUNGRY TO ANSWER GOD'S CALL

A lot of what I've done in my life has been searching for that ever elusive call of God. These days I'm sure of my calling, at least for this season of my life. I am a Christian weight loss coach, author and speaker. I guard that calling by stewarding my time and energy to be able to participate in this mission. I invite God to be God and add to or take away from what I am doing at any point in time.

I've always admired folks who knew exactly what God wanted them to be, then got training and stepped right off the college platform and into their life mission. I've learned these people are few and far between. Most of us struggle with what the purpose or meaning of our lives really is or should be. We search high and low for God's will when we need to be searching for Him. If we stay close to Him and walk in His ways, we will be in His will in everything we do.

From an early age I had hints of my calling, road signs along my journey. I view this like the imaginal cells that God places inside the caterpillar. The worm crawling on the ground carries inside it the design to become a butterfly. After it's eaten it's fill of leaves the time comes for it to go into the chrysalis. In that place everything caterpillar melts except for the imaginal cells that carry the design of the butterfly. Somehow, the caterpillar knows it has a destiny to become something more than a worm whose main purpose is eating everything in sight.

This is also my story. I was a caterpillar. The hints, road signs of God's design were always resident in me. It just took time for them to be put to use to create the new creature I was designed by God to be. I had to surrender to His design. That took a lot of time and a lot of giving up of the things I was giving in to.

BORN TO WRITE

I was born to write. By third grade I had what is called a writing callous on my right hand's middle finger where I held my pencil. I actually enjoyed essay tests even into college. I could always ace an essay test above any multiple choice version.

When I express myself through writing, I can get lost in the words. As Author James Michener so eloquently puts it, "I love writing. I love the swirl and swing of words as they tangle with human emotions." I know I have done my job when someone tells me something I wrote made them laugh, cry or think. My goal is to leave the reader changed in some way. These are all hints and shouts of the calling God gave me when He created me and knit me together in my mother's womb.[1]

His desire for me and for you is that we "might have and enjoy life, and have it in abundance to the full, until it overflows."[2] However, there is a huge stumbling block to us obtaining this. We have an enemy, a thief, who also has a mission. That mission is to steal, kill or destroy[3] my destiny and the destinies of all God's children.

OBSTACLES

There is good news and bad news about that. Satan is powerless unless we give the keys of our lives over to him. Most of us don't knowingly give him access to our home. That place is supposed to be reserved for the Holy Spirit.

"Haven't you heard yet that your body is the home of the Holy Spirit God gave you, and that He lives within you? Your own body does not belong to you. For God has bought you with a great price. So use every part of your body to give glory back to God because he owns it."[4]

God owns us, but allows us to steward our time, resources and our bodies. We have freedom of choice given to us by our Master. That gives the evil one full reign to tempt us. God tells us He will help us in our times of temptation.[5] Many times, though, I didn't want His help. I wanted to give in to temptation. I willfully did that time and time again.

> Satan is powerless unless we give the keys of our lives over to him.

As a child I knew I would one day write a book. At that point in time I wouldn't have termed it a "calling." I would have said it was a dream of mine, but it never went away. It followed me throughout my life. The dream became better defined as

I started my career in journalism. I wanted to write a true story about how someone was changed by the power of God. I wanted it to be a book that would make a difference.

Little did I know, that dream would begin by me writing my own life story, *Sweet Grace: How I Lost 250 Pounds and Stopped Trying to Earn God's Favor.*[6] When I was dreaming about writing a book and mapping out my life plan, weighing 430 pounds was never a part of that picture. I don't think it was God's plan either. I fell into the evil one's tempting snare of delicious foods, which became an addiction and nearly took my life. The devil was laughing the whole way through.

> God had this calling on my life all along, but first I had to come through the fire.

What Satan meant for evil, though, God used for His good.[7] God, in His grace and mercy, was faithful to keep calling me back to Him and the path He had for me.

During a prayer time in January of 2013, God showed me it was time for me to write the book. I was more surprised than anyone that the book was to be my story. I had gone through hell and back. I'd gained an enormous amount of weight and then lost it. Thinking about writing a true story about my biggest mess in life made me feel naked, exposed and very vulnerable.

God had this calling on my life all along, but first I had to come through the fire. My temptation time was over 30 years long. I wasn't as quick to understand that temptation comes before a person can step into his or her calling. Jesus got that memo, though, because He came through His temptations with flying colors. His the first one was similar to what got me stuck for 30 years. It took Jesus no time at all to overcome it.

He had fasted for 40 days and He was hungry.[8] I would have been more than hungry. I would have been ravenous by the evening of day one. The devil told Him to change the stones on the ground into loaves of bread to prove that He was the Son of God. Jesus gave a profound answer.

"It has been written, 'Man shall not live and be upheld and sustained by bread alone, but by every word that comes from the mouth of God.'"[9]

The Message says, "It takes more than bread to stay alive. It takes a steady stream of words from God's mouth."[10] Another version puts it this way, "No! For the Scriptures tell us that bread won't feed men's souls. Obedience to every word of God is what we need."[11]

Jesus did not even entertain the idea of giving into His physical hunger. In that one answer to the devil, He summed up why we need to have a constant, sweet hunger for God. God feeds our souls. He keeps us alive. He sustains us. Obedience to Him helps us move and navigate through our lives.

GOD'S PROCLAMATION

This scenario happened after Father God publicly singled out Jesus, effectively calling Him into the ministry Jesus knew He was to have. It was during the time He was baptized by John. When He came up out of the water and the skies opened. He saw God's Spirit descending like a dove and landing on Him.

"And suddenly a voice came from Heaven saying, 'This is My beloved Son, in whom I am well pleased.'"[12]

What a monumental occasion. Father God had just declared Jesus the One and only Son of God, Savior of the World. This was like telling the people who were listening, "Here is your King!"

There should have been a parade or a coronation. Instead, Jesus was immediately led or guided by the Holy Spirit into the wilderness to be tempted, tested and tried by the devil.[13]

Who He was didn't keep Him from temptation.

Jesus knew there was no turning back on His mission to save the world and all of mankind. He was God in human form with the backing of the God of the Universe. In His humanity, He had to go through testing to understand He must still rely on the Father to guide Him through the countdown to the cross.

It had been a red-letter day for Jesus, a mountaintop experience in His life. What better time to be tested than when He had just been given the declaration of God's favor, authority and the keys to Heaven? Now, He was ready to be tested.

Who He was didn't keep Him from temptation. It necessitated He be tempted. God allowed Satan to tempt Him at a time when He was at the height of His glory. He drew strength from that experience in order to enter into a time of temptation.

Jesus had just been called into His destiny. He knew it wasn't going to be an easy journey. He needed strength. He needed to know that even at His weakest He had the power of God to resist and overcome evil. It would bode Him well for the next three years as He stepped into what He was put here on earth to do.

MOMENTS OF GLORY TO DEPTHS OF DESPAIR

In our lives there are glorious times when we hear God and feel His anointing power guiding us into our calling. The strength of that calling will be tested. Will we endure the temptation, trial or test or will we give up and abandon our call?

The only thing that will get us through is to understand how important it is to hang on to God's promises. Even if we fail and give into temptation that doesn't mean our calling is revoked. It just means God has to tweak the timeline.

The devil had been observing Jesus. He saw Him come up out of the waters. He heard the voice from Heaven. He saw the Holy Spirit descend. More than anything this was the Father's way of saying, "Game on, Satan."

> It was the Father's way of saying, "Game on, Satan."

Jesus hadn't eaten in 40 days and nights and Satan was well aware of this fact. He came to Him at His weakest to take advantage of His situation. If he did that to Jesus, he will do the same to us. Like the first Adam,[14] we will give in to temptation and thwart our destinies if we aren't totally dependent and observant of God's presence in our lives each and every moment of every day.

Many times, it didn't take much for Satan to tempt me. I was a sugar and comfort food addict. He knew that just by observing what I was doing. He is like the retargeting ads that follow us around the internet when we even look at something we might consider purchasing.

The evil one will show us our preferences because He knows what we like. He does this not by reading our minds, but by reading our actions. He doesn't have to tempt us so much as just keep feeding us what we have already proven by our habits that we want. We keep eating out of Satan's hands ... literally.

GOD'S PLAN

God, though, out of His supreme love for us had a plan to save us. It was a plan to introduce the last Adam[15] into the world, the One who would reverse the wrongs done by the first Adam who gave into temptation without a second thought.

Realizing I have the power of the Holy Spirit who longs to help, teach and comfort me will give me victory over my temptations. Knowing Jesus understands and survived the worst kind of temptation where food is concerned helps me run to Him instead of the things I crave.

His temptation was indicative of the fleshy temptations we are faced with every single day, such as eating too much, drinking in excess, spending ourselves into debt, giving in to sexual sin or pornography, succumbing to outbursts of anger and deep places of desperation or giving ourselves over to any type of addiction.

The Bible tells us how to overcome these temptations. God's words are a weapon, a sword[16] to defeat Satan. We can wield them to fend him off. They are also life to us. Obedience to God's ways gives us purpose. No addiction satisfies like obedience.

STRONGHOLDS

As Christians we have all fallen into temptation and found ourselves being controlled by something other than God. When we do that, we step into bondage. We step into addiction, which becomes a stronghold.

A stronghold is a fortification. It is used many times in scripture to indicate the stronghold of God. The Lord is good, "a stronghold in the day of trouble and He knows those who take refuge in Him."[17] God is "my only rock and my salvation, my stronghold. I shall not be shaken."[18] These are all positive aspects of allowing God to be our stronghold.

Satan is after our destinies.

The word, though, is also used to indicate a stronghold of the evil one. In this case it means we have allowed the devil a foothold and he has created a stronghold in our lives.

"We are human, but we don't wage war as humans do. We use God's mighty weapons, not worldly weapons, to knock down the strongholds of human reasoning and to destroy false arguments. We destroy every proud obstacle that keeps people from knowing God. We capture their rebellious thoughts and teach them to obey Christ."[19]

Satan is after our destinies. He attempts to worm his way into the very stronghold we have made for God. God wants us to choose Him. God will fight for us if we want Him to. If we choose Satan's temptations, God does not scream and yell at us. He gently woos us back.

The evil one can't literally kill us, but He can tempt us to eat ourselves into an early grave and all kinds of health challenges, which will destroy our effectiveness.

Then, he can steal our destinies by making us think someone else would be better at it than we would at the assignment God has given us.

APPLICATION

God has a purpose for each of us. It started before we were born when He planned every part of us and wrote the book about our lives.[20] He wants us to succeed even more than we do. He is the one who knows exactly what we are uniquely designed to do.

"We have become His poetry, a recreated people who will fulfill the destiny He has given each of us, for we are joined to Jesus, the Anointed One. Even before we were born, God planned in advance our destiny and the good works we would do to fulfill it."[21]

I'm more hungry than ever to answer God's call on my life and to surrender to the unique design He created for me and me alone. My hope is we all are.

What we truly believe will be seen in our behaviors. Being hungry to answer His call begins with showing God by our actions that we choose Him alone. He is all we need.

There's only one person with my exact DNA. I am the only one who can raise my child, be an awesome spouse, write that special book, complete the exact job or role, teach and coach others to their victories and just be me. Others might do something similar. Others might fill in, but it is my job. We can't let the devil's temptations steal, kill or destroy our effectiveness in the Kingdom for the price of a cookie. We are worth more than that. God's Kingdom is worth more than that.

Questions:

1. What were some hints or road signs God gave you that might indicate your calling? What did you love to do as a child?

_____

_____

_____

2. What have been some obstacles to your calling? In what way has Satan tried to steal, kill or destroy your destiny?

_____

_____

_____

3. If your body is the home of the Holy Spirit, in what ways are you stewarding that resource? In what ways are you not? See 1 Cor. 6:19-20.

_____

_____

4. How has God helped you in your time of temptation? Has He given you a way out? Did you take it? Why or why not? See 1 Cor. 10:13.

_____

_____

_____

5. In what ways has giving into temptation kept you from stepping into your calling or even discovering your calling?

_____

_____

_____

6. Why is Jesus' first temptation so important? What had Jesus learned that we also need to learn? How do you see that truth impacting your life? See Matthew 4:4 NIV, MSG and TLB.

_____

_____

_____

7. Describe Jesus' calling. How did He know He was called? How do you think He felt that day? See Matt. 3:17.

_____

_____

_____

8. What tempts you the most? How does Satan know how and with what to tempt you?

_____

_____

_____

9. What does God say about your destiny? Do you have one? What things do you know which are part of your destiny? Brainstorm and list all possibilities that come to mind.

_____

_____

_____

Activity

SCRIPTURE: "You saw me before I was born. Every day of my life was recorded in your book. Every moment was laid out before a single day had passed." —Psalm 139:16 NLT

SUPPLIES: Pen

LIFE MISSION STATEMENT: We all need mission statements to guide our lives. Many times, though, we aren't aware of the deepest desires of our hearts. This exercise will help you define what those are. We will go through each part of a life mission statement so you can create your own. What follows is my Life Mission Statement. Yours should be uniquely yours. Mine is just for example

Teresa's Mission Statement:

I am a whole, healthy, happy woman administering grace and truth in a powerful way.

Notice that my statement is specific and yet, general as well. It includes several pieces I want you to think about for yourself.

I am a whole, healthy, happy woman. I made this as a prophetic life mission statement back in 1994 when I weighed 430 pounds. This is what I wanted to be. At its core it says who I am. I am a woman. That's a given, however the important thing is to say what type of woman I want to be in order to fulfill God's call on my life.

ADJECTIVES:

Choose several positive, directional adjectives you'd like to define you. I've included a list to get you started thinking. Circle words that really reach out and grab you, then keep paring your list down until you get the three. Star those.

Active	Daring	Gentle
Adventurous	Decisive	Good
Ambitious	Diligent	Graceful
Amiable	Dynamic	Happy
Boisterous	Energetic	Hard-working
Brave	Enthusiastic	Healed
Bright	Faithful	Healthy
Calm	Favored	Helpful
Compassionate	Fearless	Holy
Complete	Free	Honest
Courageous	Friendly	Imaginative
Creative	Generous	Independent
Intelligent	Practical	Sociable
Inventive	Quick-witted	Surrendered
Joy-filled	Quiet	Thoughtful
Kind	Reasonable	Trustworthy
Loving	Reliable	Truthful
Loyal	Resourceful	Understanding
Merciful	Self-Confident	Unselfish
Optimistic	Self-Controlled	Whole
Passionate	Self-Disciplined	Willing
Patient	Sensible	Zealous
Peaceful	Sensitive	Other:_____
Powerful	Sincere	_____

Write your adjectives here

_____

_____

NOUN

Nouns are people, places or things. Choose the noun to describe who you are. Most choose man or woman, but there may be a different role you want to emphasize such as mother, father, etc. Write the noun here: _____

ACTION PHRASE

My action phrase is "administering grace and truth in a powerful way." The phrase is comprised of a verb (administering), two core value nouns (grace and truth) which describe what I am administering and another adjective and noun to describe how I do that (in a powerful way).

VERB

My main verb is administering. Your verb should be one which allows God to enlarge your vision. Leave room for yourself to grow. There are many verbs you can use. Here are a list of some. Circle the ones that speak to you as you go through the list. Then choose the one which speaks loudest to you. This is the main action you are taking.

Accelerating
Advancing
Amplifying
Administering
Advising
Advocating
Authoring
Building
Catching
Clarifying
Coaching
Comforting
Composing
Coordinating
Corresponding
Counseling
Creating
Delivering
Defining
Designing
Developing
Devising
Diagnosing
Discipling
Editing
Educating
Enabling
Encouraging

Enhancing
Establishing
Expanding
Expediting
Facilitating
Fostering
Furthering
Gaining
Generating
Guiding
Helping
Identifying
Illustrating
Implementing
Improving
Incorporating
Informing
Initiating
Inspiring
Instituting
Interpreting
Introducing
Investigating
Joining
Keeping
Launching
Lifting
Managing

Maximizing
Mentoring
Mobilizing
Motivating
Navigating
Organizing
Planning
Praying
Producing
Promoting
Reconciling
Refining
Refocusing
Rehabilitating
Relocating
Revitalizing
Shaping
Simplifying
Strengthening
Sustaining
Teaching
Training
Transforming
Unifying
Writing
Other: _____

_____

Write your verb here: _____

CORE VALUE NOUNS

What do I want to administer? These nouns are bit different. They really denote your core values. They must come from inside you. What message are you sharing? What is it you want people to understand? For me the marriage of the compassionate nature of grace and the reality of truth is what I want to share.

Here are some core values. Circle those that speak the loudest to you. This list may help you think of others you could use. This is not an exhaustive list, but it will help you get started. Pare down your list to two.

Accountability	Goodness	Perseverance
Authenticity	Grace	Personal Growth
Boldness	Growth	Prayer
Character	Honesty	Purity
Confidence	Honor	Reliability
Courage	Hope	Respect
Creativity	Humility	Self-Control
Devotion	Humor	Selflessness
Discipleship	Intimacy	Steadfastness
Discipline	Joy	Submission
Efficiency	Justice	Teachable Spirit
Encouragement	Kindness	Teamwork
Endurance	Leadership	Transparency
Enthusiasm	Learning	Truth
Evangelism	Mercy	Unity
Excellence	Obedience	Wisdom
Faith	Passion	Worship
Family	Patience	Zeal

Write your two or three core value nouns here:

_____

_____

_____

HOW

How do you share your passion? Do you preach, teach, sing, write, draw, counsel, coach? I could have said by writing, coaching and speaking. Those would be verbs and would show action. This is a great way to end my mission statement, but it would limit me to just those things.

When I wrote my mission statement coaching and speaking were not even on my mind. I could have just used writing, but I knew that wasn't all I would be doing.

I began to ask, "What do I want the outcome of my life mission to be?" This enlarged my thinking and my possibilities. Then, I asked God to really lead me to the word to define what He wanted me to be about.

Answer these questions.

1. What vehicle will I use to express my life mission?

_____

_____

_____

2. How do I want people who are impacted to feel?

_____

_____

_____

3. What do I want them to do as a result of my life mission?

_____

_____

_____

Answering these questions will complete the ending of your mission statement. Now put everything together in your own life mission statement.

I am a whole, healthy, happy (all adjectives) woman (noun), administering (positive action verb) grace and truth (core value nouns) in a powerful way (how statement).

You can use this format or develop one of your own. Now, write that down under Your Life Mission Statement.

Don't be afraid to adjust your mission statement as you learn more about yourself. However, it is amazing how most everything I do or have dreams of doing fits within the scope of my life mission statement.

My Life Mission Statement

More Inspiration

Magazines are great places to garner inspiration if you are more visual in how you understand life. Gather magazines of all types for this exercise. As you find a headline, a word or picture that inspires you, tear it out and put it in a pile. When you have a good pile.

Stop and see what you have. Toss aside those items that don't speak to you. There may be something about a picture that states a core value such as excellence, beauty, peacefulness or creativity. Note this.

Now what speaks to you from this? Organize the words or thoughts into a statement. Adjust it until you have what you sense God is showing you.

You can also paste these words and pictures on a poster or heavy paper to make a Vision Board to remember your Life Mission Statement.

ENDNOTES

1. Psalm 139:13 NLT
2. John 10:10 AMP
3. John 10:10 AMP
4. 1 Corinthians 6:19-20 TLB
5. 1 Corinthians 10:13 NLT
6. Teresa's book, *Sweet Grace: How I Lost 250 Pounds and Stopped Trying to Earn God's Favor*, is available on Amazon in print, kindle or audible.
7. Romans 8:28 NIV, Gen. 50:20 NASB
8. Matthew 4:2 NIV
9. Matthew 4:4 AMP
10. Matthew 4:4 MSG
11. Matthew 4:4 TLB
12. Matthew 3:17 NIV
13. Matthew 4:1 AMP
14. Genesis 3:6 NIV
15. 2 Cor. 15:45 NIV
16. Ephesians 6:17 NIV
17. Nahum 1:7 NASB
18. Psalm 62:6 NASB
19. 2 Corinthians 10:3-5 NLT
20. Psalm 139:16 NLT
21. Ephesians 2:10 TPT

"We are God's poetry, a
recreated people who
will fulfill the destiny He
has given each of us for
we are joined to Jesus,
the Anointed One. Even
before we were born God
planned in advance our
destiny and the good works
we would do to fulfill it."

EPHESIANS 2:10 TPT

FINAL WORD
FROM TERESA

''ve loved traveling with you on this journey. The only thing better would be if we could be in a room together sharing our thoughts and ideas around the topics in this book. We all have different journeys. Mine, for as far back as I can remember has involved food in some way or another. I had allowed food to become my god. It is a sad, but very true fact.

"Their destiny is destruction, their god is their stomach, and their glory is in their shame. Their mind is set on earthly things. But our citizenship is in heaven. And we eagerly await a Savior from there, the Lord Jesus Christ."[1]

> Their god is their stomach, and their glory is in their shame.

If you knew me when I weighed 430 pounds then you know the absolute truth of this. In reality, you only need look at my before and after pictures to understand how much sugar addiction affected every part of my life.

I had so many couldn'ts in my life all because of my size. I couldn't walk across the store without sitting down. I couldn't go to the mall without driving round and round until I found a close place to park. I couldn't sit in a booth at a restaurant. I couldn't eat just a normal helping of anything. I couldn't go an hour without eating something. I couldn't stay awake all day and I couldn't get a good night's sleep. I couldn't even attempt to go to sleep at night without my oxygen machine. I couldn't walk without pain. I couldn't ride in a normal car. I couldn't work an 8-5 job. I couldn't sit in a folding chair for fear it would collapse. I couldn't sit in any kind of normal living room chair or couch because I couldn't get up from it without help. I couldn't find clothes in my size.

> I was like an alcoholic only with foods made with sugar and flour.

I couldn't. I couldn't. I couldn't. I couldn't. I couldn't. I couldn't. You get the idea. It was frustrating and yet, I still continued to overeat.

Food was my go-to source to feel comfort, relief from emotional turmoil, protection from all life would throw at me. Foods, especially foods made with sugar and flour, gave me pleasure and made me happy for the short period of time after I ate them. They gave me that sugar high and then I would crash until I got some more to make me feel that same way again.

I was addicted. I was like an alcoholic only with foods made with sugar and flour. To get free I had to stop using my drug of choice. I had to stop pleasing the god of my stomach.

I had exhausted all my resources, pulled out all the tricks known to medical science when I finally decided to try things God's way. Back in 1977, He told me what to do. He said, "Stop eating sugar. Eat more meats, fruits and vegetables and stop eating so much bread."

I knew it was the answer, but I could never sustain it. When I owned the fact that I am a sugar addict and laid that weakness at His feet, God in His grace stepped in with all His power to help me go forward.

He placed me in a group with a mentor who could lead me to freedom from my self-imposed tomb of sugar addiction. I call him another. Peers like myself, who were facing the same challenges as I was, I call "others". They helped encourage, commensurate and prod me. With another and others, I still needed "the Other," the power of God to sustain and empower me. With that kind of group I was able to go forward on my journey because His grace is enough. His power is made complete[2] when I admit my weakness and lay it down at His feet.

PHENOMENAL THINGS

After losing the weight, phenomenal things began to happen. God called me to write *Sweet Grace*. I knew nothing about self-publishing, but He led me to resources to help me. I was overwhelmed when I discovered *Sweet Grace* was the #1 Christian Weight Loss Memoir on Amazon and, as far as I know, it still is.

Since then I've written *Sweet Change: True Stories of Transformation* about the lifestyle change journey we all must take to really become new creations[3] in Him.

The real issue those who go on a weight loss journey face is not only losing the weight, but keeping it off. My book, *Sweet Freedom,* is all about dealing with that issue, which involves confronting lies we believe, dealing with our emotions and experiencing God's truth in the midst of the sometimes dark and scary things in our past. *Sweet Freedom Study Guide* gives principles and tools to help us get through some of these issues.

ENTER WEIGHT LOSS COACHING

Perhaps some of the most fulfilling opportunities I've had are leading several Christian weight loss coaching groups. Coaching wasn't something I particularly wanted to do because I knew I'd have to deal with every excuse in the book. Still, I think that's exactly one reason God called me to do it. I know the excuses and I know how He led me through them.

After writing *Sweet Grace* I got more emails, messages and Facebook comments than I could possibly answer. Many wanted to tell me their story and wanted my help. I found I was giving many of the same answers to each, but I didn't have the ability to form an ongoing relationship, which I knew they needed in order to walk out this journey.

When God showed me I was to begin coaching, I knew the only way I could help many individuals at the same time was through a closed private Facebook group. Now that group has morphed into much more than just getting together to talk.

Thousands of pounds of weight have been lost in this group. Success stories abound like Rhonda Burrows, who at 4'10" has lost 60 pounds. Many others have lost that much or more. Better than the weight loss, they have finally learned the secret God wants all of us to embrace: When we fix our attention on Him we will be changed from the inside out.[4]

I don't believe there is a one-size fits all eating plan. There are some tried and true principles that work, especially for those who know they are sugar addicts. The free course, #KickSugar, is a starter course for those principles. It's 10 short videos and yes, it really is free.

Our starter group is #KickWeight, a six-month coaching class. We open it for about a month and close it as the members go through the course content together. It is really a one of a kind Christian weight loss program. Sign up on the wait list to be notified when the next course starts. I love the process. The first two #KickWeight groups lost more than 1,000 pounds together.

> When we fix our attention on Him, we will be changed from the inside out.

When we begin to get our focus on the right thing and make a firm commitment, not to a diet, but to allowing God to lead us, amazing things happen.

Sweet Change is the coaching group which has been going monthly since 2014. It is an ongoing group with access to over 100 of my teaching videos and courses, along with new video teaching each week, a monthly video call and direct mentoring and coaching from me. I help people through the pitfalls they keep encountering, aid in inner healing and give practical, emotional and spiritual advise.

My heart's cry is to help those who want to get free from what's holding them back from living their best life now. I learned on my journey that if I really wanted help I had to invest in myself to make those necessary changes. I require those in my groups to make an investment of commitment, thought, resources and intentional, dedicated time with God.

What's holding you back from living your best life now?

For those who really want to go forward with whatever is keeping them stuck, VIP Freedom Coaching is tailor-made for them. I say that because it is the only group in which I do one-on-one inner healing coaching. I also teach these principles. After completing this three-month intensive, participants will receive a certificate showing they have taken this course. Additional one-on-one coaching packages will still be available if they so choose.

SPEAKING

It was never been my dream to be a speaker. After I wrote *Sweet Grace,* God opened doors for me to be interviewed on Christian television. I dragged my feet when the first call came in inviting me to be on a live show with two 15-minute segments. I chose to be on a five-minute tv news spot first.

When I didn't die or sit and stare blankly at the camera, I decided to try the longer segments. Now I've been done too many to count. Visit the press tab on my website if you're interested in watching some of the shows or listening to the radio interviews and podcasts. I have more to add when there's a moment, which there rarely is.

I share where I'm at because I see all of this the development of understanding more of my destiny. None of happened until I began to walk in obedience to what God had shown me to do regarding my health. I always thought my biggest problem was my weight. That was just the tip of the iceberg.

> The bondage of my past was comfort foods.

Life didn't fall into place for me because I lost weight. The physical pounds were not my biggest problem. The fact that I didn't fully trust God to lead me on my journey was my biggest problem. I wasn't obedient to His voice because I thought I knew more than He did.

I didn't listen to what He told me back in 1977 until it was almost too late. Even after being obedient, I had to be willing to allow God to uncover some of the deep emotional issues that led to spiritual lies I believed. I had to allow Him to do the deep change work in me that is never, ever pretty, but so necessary.

What God wants for us, more than anything else, is that we be set "free, not partially, but wonderfully and completely free. Let us always cherish this truth and stubbornly refuse to go back to the bondage of our past."[5]

I never have to stop and wonder what the bondage of my past was and still can be if I let it. It's comfort foods, plain and simple. I had a relationship with food like I would with a good friend, although the sugary foods I craved were not a good friend to me. They were the lying, manipulating, conniving, back-stabbing kind, all the while whispering words of love and comfort, but slowly and surely killing me. It's interesting how we can be lulled into denial by a substance in much the same as a controlling person.

God uses the analogy of food to let us know that He longs for us to crave Him more than we crave a cookie, turtle brownie, cheesecake or Mamaw's oatmeal cake. We must develop an appetite for Him. We must hunger and thirst for God[6] above all other things because only then can we be filled to overflowing.

Remember those people who were making their stomach their god and setting their minds on earthly things, things they could smell, see, taste and touch?

Paul also told them, "There's far more to life for us. We're citizens of high heaven! We're waiting the arrival of the Savior, the Master, Jesus Christ, who will transform our earthy bodies into glorious bodies like his own. He'll make us beautiful and whole with the same powerful skill by which He is putting everything as it should be, under and around Him."[7]

GOD ALWAYS GIVES US A CHOICE

We do have a choice. God always gives us a choice. We can focus on temporal things or we can focus on eternal, forever things. Focusing on our relationship with God, worship, praise, adoration and obedience is the only way to live life in the abundance He has promised us.[8]

Then He will lead us to begin to fulfill in even greater measure the destiny He has given each of us. He, indeed, has plans for our good, not for our disaster. They are plans to give us a future and a hope.[9]

Once again, thank you for choosing to take this journey with me. Please continue to connect with me through email, Facebook, Twitter, Instagram, Pinterest and my website. Everything is listed at the back of this book in the Products and Resources section.

GIFTS FOR YOU

We have gifts for you over at TeresaShieldsParker.com. Take any or all. They are under the free tab. Don't miss all the products I've mentioned, including *Sweet Hunger* teaching videos, and the free *Sweet Hunger Leader's Guide*, over on my website. Get the exact url to grab the leader's guide on next page. You can purchase a downloadable version of *Sweet Hunger* to print and use in notebook for easier writing over on my website.

Finally, please take a minute and tell us what you liked about the study and what kinds of studies you'd like to see from us in the future.

I'd love to know if you did the study on your own or in group. How many were in the group? What was the best thing about the study? How would you change the study? If you used the *Sweet Hunger* video teachings were they helpful? What about the discussion questions and activities? Were they helpful? Which activity did your group or you enjoy the most? Contact me at info@TeresaShieldsParker.com.

Sweet Grace for Your Journey

Teresa

ENDNOTES

1. Philippians 3:19-20 NIV
2. 2 Corinthians 12:9 MSG (Teresa's version)
3. 2 Corinthians 5:17 NLT
4. Romans 12:2 MSG
5. Galatians 5:1 TPT
6. Matthew 5:6 NIV
7. Philippians 3:20-21 MSG
8. John 10:10 NIV
9. Jeremiah 29:11 NLT

PRODUCTS & RESOURCES

SWEET HUNGER LEADER'S GUIDE
AND VIDEO TEACHINGS

The *Sweet Hunger Leader's Guide* is FREE with the purchase of this book. Simply go the url below to download your copy. Do not search for it because it will not show up on the search option. It is FREE for those who have a copy of the book because you are special. The Guide is only accessed with this exact url:

https://TeresaShieldsParker.com/Sweet-Hunger-Guide/

The *Sweet Hunger* video teaching series includes nine video teachings by Teresa Shields Parker. They run between 18 and 28 minutes long. In them Teresa teaches each chapter and the introduction. They work great for personal or group study. They can be purchased at https://TeresaShieldsParker.com/Sweet-Hunger-Videos/

If you'd like to purchase a downloadable .pdf copy of *Sweet Hunger* go to the books tab on her website.

SWEET GRACE

In *Sweet Grace: How I Lost 250 Pounds and Stopped Trying To Earn God's Favor* Teresa chronicles her physical journey of walking out of sugar addiction by the grace and power of God.

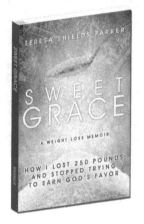

She shares honestly and transparently about what it is like to be super morbidly obese and what it takes to turn around and become free.

Get your copy in print, kindle or audiobook on Amazon or ebook on her website. Add *Sweet Grace Study Guide* to use in conjunction with *Sweet Grace* for personal or group study.

SWEET CHANGE

Sweet Change: True Stories of Transformation is all about the power of change and how to tap into it.

Teresa shares stories of individuals who have found their own personal ingredients work great with God's power in order to lose weight and step into total transformation—body, soul and spirit. Get your copy on Amazon today in print or kindle. Or on her website in ebook.

SWEET FREEDOM

In *Sweet Freedom: Losing Weight and Keeping It Off With God's Help,* Teresa shares her journey through emotional issues which kept 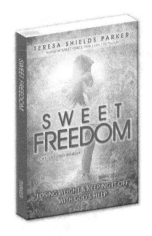 her bound in sugar addiction for years. Teresa discusses keys to identifying and eradicating the emotional issues which can become spiritual lies.

These surface as presenting issues or excuses which hold us back in accomplishing any great endeavor whether it be starting a new career, overcoming an addictive habit, noticing our tendency to get into bad relationships, giving into fits of rage or anger or trying time and time again to lose weight. Teresa uses her experience with extreme weight loss to illustrate these Freedom principles.

SWEET FREEDOM STUDY GUIDE

Sweet Freedom Study Guide is a necessary companion to *Sweet Freedom*. Once you read *Sweet Freedom*, you will want to understand the concepts, tools and processes Teresa used to help her on her journey to freedom from food addiction. The study guide also includes a chapter-by-chapter study guide with questions, activities and other information to make your group study successful. It is  available on Amazon in print and on Teresa's website in ebook.

SWEET CHANGE CHRISTIAN WEIGHT LOSS COACHING GROUP

After losing over 260 pounds, Teresa felt the call to help others overcome their food addictions. In 2014 she began Sweet Change Christian Weight Loss Coaching Group.

This ongoing monthly group includes weekly teaching videos, monthly video call, private Facebook group, direct coaching from Teresa and access at any time to her video vault with over 100 videos and more being added all the time.

These teaching videos are short courses with study guides and action steps. To lean more go to https://TeresaShieldsParker. com/Sweet-Change/. Join any time.

#KICKWEIGHT

#KickWeight is Teresa's low-cost introductory six-month weight loss course designed to help individuals ditch the diet mentality and step into the total surrender of a lifestyle change. It opens twice a year for new members. To be notified of the next group put your name on the wait list at https://TeresaShieldsParker.com/KickWeight.

VIP FREEDOM COACHING

VIP Freedom Coaching is for those who want to go on a spiritual transformation journey through one-on-one sessions with Teresa. This is her executive option for those who mean business! Includes six personal sessions with Coach Teresa via video or phone call over three months. The teaching element will explain the various principles used during coaching sessions. A certificate of completion will be given for those who finish this journey.

Limited in number, this group is for those who are ready to shake off self-limiting beliefs, face their false self and go forward into the destiny God has for them. It can include Christian weight loss, but Teresa will help you with whatever issues come to the surface. For more information, go to: https://TeresaShieldsParker.com/VIP-Freedom-Coaching/.

GIVE THE GIFT OF COACHING

Give the gift of a coaching to a friend. Join the program and pay with your card either monthly or in full. Send an email to info@TeresaShieldsParker.com with name and email of the person you joined for and your name and email.

Teresa Shields Parker with husband, Roy

CONNECT WITH TERESA

WEBSITE: TeresaShieldsParker.com

EMAIL: Info@TeresaShieldsParker.com

Amazon: Amazon.com/author/TeresaShieldsParker

Facebook: Facebook.com/TeresaShieldsParker

Twitter: Twitter.com/treeparker

Instagram: Instagram.com/treeparker

CPSIA information can be obtained
at www.ICGtesting.com
Printed in the USA
FSHW020804170219
55735FS